C000161164

Traditional
Chinese
Folktales

中國民間故事

Traditional Chinese Folktales

Yin-lien C.
Chin

Yetta S.
Center

Mildred
Ross

Illustrations by Lu Wang

NORTH CASTLE BOOKS
Armonk, New York
London, England

First trade edition, 1996

Copyright © 1989 by M. E. Sharpe, Inc.

All rights reserved. No part of this book may be reproduced in any form
without written permission from the publisher, M. E. Sharpe, Inc.,
80 Business Park Drive, Armonk, New York 10504.

Library of Congress Cataloging-in-Publication Data

Chinese folktales : an anthology / Yin-lien C. Chin,
Yetta S. Center, Mildred Ross : illustrations by Lu Wang
p.   cm.
Originally published : Traditional Chinese folktales, 1989.
"A North castle book."
ISBN 1-56324-800-X (pbk. : alk. paper)
1. Tales—China. 2. Folklore—China. I. Chin, Yin-lien C
II. Center, Yetta S.   III. Ross, Mildred.
GR335.C5553   1996
398.2′0951—dc20   96-5158
CIP
Printed in the United States of America

The paper used in this publication meets the minimum requirements of
American National Standard for Information Sciences—
Permanence of Paper for Printed Library Materials,
ANSI Z 39.48-1984.

EB (p)   10   9   8   7   6   5   4

North Castle Books
An imprint of M. E. Sharpe, Inc.

For: Ann, Arielle, Bonnie,
David, Jennifer, Shana, Sharon,
Thomas, and Zena

Contents

Preface

The folktales chosen for this collection, all old favorites, provide the reader with a glimpse of Chinese life whose culture and traditions date back over thousands of years. Abounding in magic and fantasy, they run the gamut from romance and adventure to historical truths.

Despite their ancient origins, the themes that appear in Chinese folktales are similar to those in the folk literature of all nations. Thus *The Golden Carp* is an early version of the Cinderella story, and the tragic fate of the lovers in *Liang Shanbo and Ju Yingtai* is reminiscent of *Romeo and Juliet*.

These stories are part of the great Chinese oral tradition that has endured down through the ages. Although most of the authors are anonymous, *Monkey* and *Finding a Wife for the River God* are exceptions. *Monkey* is based on an excerpt from a famous sixteenth century novel by Wu Cheng-en. *Finding a Wife for the River God* is based on the book *Shr Ji*, written by the noted historian Sz-Ma Chyan during the Han dynasty.

Each selection has been translated from the original Chinese, but some liberties were taken in the interest of clarity and readability. The transliteration of Chinese names is based on the Yale system, which offers the easiest phonetic pronunciation for readers of English. We hope that the tales will enrich, entertain, and delight.

Traditional Chinese Folktales

The
Clever
Daughter-
in-Law

Were it not that his three sons were so stupid, Jang Guo-lau would have been the envy of everyone in his neighborhood. He was a prosperous merchant whose tea shop was crowded with customers every day. When he was carried through the streets in his beautiful sedan chair, people turned their heads to stare. True, he was the father of three sons, which would have been considered the greatest of blessings. Instead, he was pitied.

Jang Guo-lau had rejoiced each time his wife gave birth to a male child, but as he watched them grow beyond boyhood into manhood, he felt himself more cursed than blessed.

The eldest was good-natured but a dullard. Everyone took advantage of him. He could not be trusted with money and could not be depended upon to carry out the simplest of errands without becoming confused.

The middle son had a quick temper and was always getting into fights. He didn't have the good sense to stay out of quarrels that often led from words to punches. The family had become accustomed to seeing him with a blackened eye, a bloody nose, or an ear puffed up by a good boxing.

The third son, though he was taller and stronger than his brothers, was lazy. Each day he slept until noon. Evenings he spent in the company of rowdy friends, often arriving home in the wee hours of the morning, besotted with wine. The only time he used his head was when he tried to think of a way to avoid his chores. Is it any wonder that Jang Guo-lau worried about what would become of his sons after his death?

When the two older boys married, Jang hoped that their wives would be able to change their bad habits. But the girls they chose as brides were raised in accordance with traditional belief that men commanded and women obeyed. They helped their mother-in-law with the household work and did as they were told without complaint. In the presence of their father-in-law and at mealtime they never looked at him directly and spoke only when spoken to, with as few words as possible.

"I have two more mouths to feed," Jang brooded, "and my burdens are even heavier than before."

When the third son became of marriageable age, Jang was determined to find a wife for him, someone who would be an asset to the family instead of just another responsibility. He sent for the village matchmaker and gave her very clear instructions.

"I want you to look for a bride for my youngest son. It is not essential that she be a beauty or that she have a wealthy father. It would not disturb me if she came from another village. I would not reject her if she were a little older than the boy. But she must be intelligent." With the offer to pay her handsomely for her troubles, he bid the matchmaker a good day.

Jang could not allay his uneasiness about the future. To find a girl with a good head who could think clearly might take a long time, longer than the measure of years still left to him. If such a girl were to be found, her parents might not consent to a marriage with his lazy son. These uncertainties weighed on his mind and kept him awake nights. While he still clung to a glimmer of hope that the matchmaker would succeed in her search, Jang decided to make plans in case she failed. He would put his two daughters-in-law to a test in order to determine which one was the more intelligent. Then he would try to teach the brighter one how to manage the family's finances. He wasn't very optimistic that his plan would succeed, but at the very least he had to make an attempt.

One day Jang summoned them both to his sitting chamber. They came at once and stood before him, eyes lowered, afraid that they had done something wrong. Instead of the harsh words they feared, he spoke to them kindly.

"You have not returned to your homes to visit your parents in many months," he began. "Would you like to spend a few days with them?"

"Oh, yes," they answered with one voice.

"Well, then, why don't you pack a few things and make ready to leave. You have worked hard for a long time and you deserve a rest," Jang added, as if he were granting them a special favor out of the goodness of his heart.

"Honorable Father," asked the older daughter-in-law, "how long may I stay?"

"You may stay from three to five days."

"How long may I stay?" the second daughter-in-law chimed in.

"You, my child," said the old man, "may stay for seven or eight days."

As they turned to leave the room, Jang called them back.

"Just one more thing. You must both leave tomorrow morning and you must both return on the very same day."

"Oh, thank you, thank you, Honorable Father." They stepped backward, bowing repeatedly, until they reached the door. Jabbering excitedly, they ran to their rooms. So delighted were they with the prospect of a few days of freedom, they never gave the slightest thought to Jang's instructions.

On the following morning they made their farewells.

"Have a very pleasant journey," Jang wished them. "And if you should desire to bring me a gift from home, I would like more than anything else to have a fire wrapped in paper."

"Certainly, Honorable Father," the older daughter-in-law agreed, barely listening to what he said. "We will do as you ask."

"Yes, yes," echoed the other daughter-in-law, "anything that will please you."

Dressed in their finest clothes, their black hair braided neatly and rolled into a bun, the two girls set off and walked briskly toward the outskirts of the city. When they reached the city gates where they had to part company, the older one suddenly stopped.

"Did our father-in-law instruct us to return on the same day?" she asked her companion. The younger girl nodded.

"How can that be?" the older one wondered aloud. "If I have permission to stay away from three to five days and you have permission to stay away for seven or eight days, how can we both return on the same day?"

Now that it was stated so clearly and logically, the younger daughter-in-law finally realized they had a problem.

"And what did he mean by a gift of fire wrapped in paper?" persisted the elder.

Asked to cope with two such difficult riddles was more than the younger girl's brain could contend with. Sick with worry, she broke down and began to cry. Soon she was joined by the older one.

The sight of two young women sobbing near the busy thoroughfare attracted the attention of passersby. Most of them just stared as they hurried along, intent on their own private affairs. But the butcher's daughter, Phoenix, on her way to market, noticed them and stopped to inquire if they were in need of help.

"May I be of assistance?" asked Phoenix. "Are you lost?"

"No," replied the older daughter-in-law. "We are not lost. It is just that we are faced with a most vexing puzzle, and, try as we may, we cannot think of a way to solve it."

"No, we cannot solve it," repeated the younger daughter-in-law, adding not a whit by her repetition.

With kindly prodding, the two girls told Phoenix their tale of woe—how their father-in-law had offered them the chance to visit their parents, how he had instructed one to stay from three to five days and the other to take seven or eight days, how he had made it clear that they were to return on the very same day, and finally, what he wished them to bring back as a gift.

Phoenix heard them out to the end. Then she smiled and said, "Do not weep any longer. Can't you see that your father-in-law was teasing you? He meant to tell you that your visit may last for fifteen days."

The girls were dumbfounded. Three to five days, seven to eight days, now fifteen days! It was too much for them to comprehend. Numbers were always so confusing. They had never been good at adding and subtracting, and as for multiplication and division, they believed only scholars could handle such complex figuring.

Patiently, Phoenix explained that when their father-in-law spoke of three to five days, he meant three times five days, which equals fifteen. When he said seven or eight days, he meant seven plus eight days, which also equals fifteen.

"So that's it," said the older daughter-in-law. "I should have figured it out for myself."

"As for the gift of fire wrapped in paper, . . ." Phoenix tried to hold back her laughter. She marveled at how childlike they were, and how naive. "Your father-in-law was asking for an ordinary lantern." Still they showed no sign of understanding. She explained again in very simple words. "Think of a lantern as a lit candle inside a paper container. Is that not a fire wrapped in paper?"

"Yes, of course, that's it! Why didn't I think of that?" said the older girl with relief. The younger one remained silent, still mulling over the tangled reasoning.

They thanked Phoenix for her kindness and hurried away. Fifteen days later they were both back at home, happy and in good cheer. They each presented their father-in-law with a colorful lantern.

Now Jang was the one who was puzzled. How had they seen through his riddles, he wanted to know. The girls looked at each other, neither one wanting to speak first. Then the younger daughter-in-law could not contain herself and blurted out the whole story.

"Well, well," thought Jang to himself. "If the butcher's daughter had enough wisdom to unravel my little joke, she must have a good head. I think I may have found a proper wife for my youngest son." He decided not to bother the matchmaker yet. He would arrange to look Phoenix over himself.

Several days later Jang walked into the butcher shop. Phoenix was busy serving another customer, and while he waited his turn, he took notice of how efficiently she worked. Besides, she was quite attractive. Her figure was slender, and when she smiled she revealed her lovely, evenly spaced, white teeth.

"May I help you, sir?" she asked in a very business-like manner.

"Yes, I would like a half pound of skin attached to skin," Jang said in a matter-of-fact tone, as if he were asking for a regular cut of meat. He watched Phoenix to see if there were any reaction.

"As you wish, sir," she said smartly and disappeared into the back room of the store. In a moment she returned and placed a pig's ear on the scale.

"Exactly one half pound, sir. Is there anything else you would like?"

"That will be all today, and thank you very much."

Jang left with his purchase. He was now convinced beyond any doubt that he had indeed found a daughter-in-law he could be proud of. Without delay he asked the matchmaker to proceed with the necessary arrangements.

Phoenix's father at first doubted that Jang's youngest son was worthy of his only daughter. The matchmaker, however, was able to convince him that Phoenix would be marrying into a wealthy family where she would want for nothing. Her husband-to-be, the matchmaker explained, was a lazy youth and there was no denying it, but with maturity he would surely outgrow his undesirable habits.

"When a man marries a good wife," she assured Phoenix's father, "she can have a strong influence over him and change him to her liking."

After the matchmaker sweetened the offer with promises of elaborate gifts for him and his daughter, the butcher gave his consent to the marriage.

From the day Phoenix came to live in her father-in-law's house, she had a marvelous effect on her husband. He began to keep regular hours and spend more time at home. At first he admired her for her pleasant, agreeable nature, then he grew to love her.

Happiest of all was Jang. His new daughter-in-law took over many of the jobs he had begun to find burdensome in his old age. Before long he felt so comfortable leaving her in charge of his shop that he would spend afternoons playing chess with his cronies or attending a show in the company of his grandson. In due time he turned over the entire management of his business and finances to Phoenix.

Jang never ceased to admire his daughter-in-law's ambition and her skill. Under her wise management the tea shop was expanded, attracting new patrons until it became the favorite gathering place in the community. The family's wealth grew far beyond the old man's expectations.

Jang was contemplating his good fortune while he sat sunning himself in the front garden of his house. He fondly recalled planting the tiny seedlings now grown to fully branched fruit trees. The tea house, the busiest for miles around, earned enough to permit his family to enjoy all sorts of luxuries. "Truly," he told himself, "I am the luckiest man alive," and he wanted to shout it to the world. On a whim he picked up a piece of dried clay with which he wrote two sentences on either side of the door frame. They read, "How many families can compete with mine? We need never ask favors from others."

Later that afternoon the local prefect, in the course of his usual rounds, happened to pass by Jang's house. The words

The local prefect happened to pass by Jang's house.

scrawled next to the door caught his eye.

"Well, there's a bit of pompous boastfulness," he thought. "Whoever thinks so highly of himself needs to be taught a lesson in humility." As soon as he returned to his office he ordered an underling to bring the owner of the house before him early the next morning.

Jang, shifting uneasily from one foot to the other, faced the haughty prefect.

"How dare you brag about not needing favors from others! Even I, a high official of the government, must sometimes appeal to others for help. If you think you are so capable, there are three things I'm sure you can do for me. First, find a calf that was born of a bull. Second, bring me enough cloth to cover the sky. Third, gather enough peanut oil to fill the ocean."

Jang felt humiliated. His tongue stuck to his palate, and he could not think of a single word in his own defense.

The prefect added a stern warning. "You have exactly one week to complete these assignments. If you fail to do so in time, you will be severely punished. Dismissed!"

Jang was led out of the room, trembling. His wonderful world had crumbled. He would lose face and be the laughingstock of the neighborhood.

Gone was his usual cheerfulness. Instead he took to lying in bed even during his waking hours, and often refused to come to the table at mealtime. On the rare occasion when he did leave his bedroom, he would pace back and forth in the garden, his brow wrinkled, his shoulders bent. It was plain to everyone that he was sorely troubled, but when they asked him what was wrong and offered to help, his reply was always, "Nothing, nothing is wrong."

The days passed slowly, days of unbearable agony for Jang. Phoenix knocked on his door one evening, calling out, "I've brought you a cup of hot tea." She waited for a reply. When none came, she nudged the door open and found him sitting in a chair, gazing absentmindedly out of the window.

"Father," she offered, "here is your favorite green tea." Jang, hands trembling, reached for the steaming cup but said nothing. Phoenix waited until he had taken a few sips before she spoke.

"We have all been made unhappy by your brooding. It is as if you were carrying all the earth's troubles on your shoulders." Jang sipped the fragrant, soothing beverage, but remained silent. She tried again. "If only you would explain the cause of your distress, I may be able to help you."

The old man set down the empty cup. The look of defeat on his face was pitiful to see. Blushing with shame, he told her of his encounter with the prefect.

"Is there a single man who walks this earth able to do what he asked of me? And now there is only one day left before I must carry out his orders or face some dreadful punishment." Jang sighed. He could see no way out of his predicament.

"Do not trouble yourself any longer," said Phoenix. "I shall go to see the prefect on your behalf. Perhaps I can persuade him to withdraw his demands, or failing that, to be lenient in his punishment."

Early the next morning Phoenix appeared at the prefect's office carrying a ruler and a ladle.

"Who are you?" he demanded gruffly. Phoenix realized immediately that she would have to deal with a minor official who suffered from an exaggerated idea of his own importance.

"Your Honor," she said with feigned humility. "I am the daughter-in-law of Jang Guo-lau, who was to report to you today on the completion of three important tasks. Unfortunately, he is about to give birth to a baby, so he sent me to tell you that he will not be able to come."

"Have you lost your mind?" shouted the prefect, the blood rising to his face. "How can a man give birth to a child?"

"Exactly, Your Excellency, a man can't give birth to a child, neither can a bull give birth to a calf."

Phoenix appeared at the prefect's office with a ruler and a ladle.

The prefect was rattled but tried to maintain his dignity. "Very well, then, have you brought enough cloth to cover the sky?"

"Ah, Your Highness," answered Phoenix with disarming sweetness, "we have more than enough cloth to do the job in our own storerooms. The only problem is that we don't know for sure how many yards are needed. I have brought this ruler, and if you can provide me with exact measurements of the length and breadth of the sky, the cloth will be delivered without delay."

The embarrassed prefect began to feel that he had met his equal in this mere slip of a girl, but he didn't know when to leave well enough alone.

"Forget the cloth," he sputtered, "but have you brought the peanut oil to fill the ocean?"

"Well, sir, here again we are confronted with some difficulty." Phoenix was enjoying the prefect's obvious discomfort. Beads of sweat had gathered on his forehead. But she never let on. Offering him the ladle, she added, "Perhaps you can ask your attendants to scoop out all the water in the ocean. Once it is empty, we shall gladly fill it with peanut oil of the finest quality."

The prefect was speechless. Fuming and fretting for the rest of the day, he canceled all official business and refused to see anyone. To think that he had been outwitted by a mere woman! It was degrading!

That evening at dinner, the whole family enjoyed a hearty laugh when Phoenix explained how she had confounded the prefect. Jang's eyes sparkled with tears of joy. He realized that of all his money and wealth, the greatest treasure he possessed was his clever daughter-in-law.

Finding
a Wife
for
the River
God

Today the little village of Ye is one of the most prosperous in all of China. It lies along a wide river that delivers abundant water to the fields of wheat and millet. The industrious villagers are well fed and content.

But this was not always so. There was a time when catastrophe struck every year. In the spring the river regularly overflowed its banks, causing death and destruction. Were it not for the wisdom of one man, nothing would ever have changed.

In the fifth century B.C., Syimen Bau, who had distinguished himself by his scholarship and intelligence, was appointed prefect of the village of Ye. It was his job to explain the government laws to the people of the village and to help make their lives more pleasant. He was a wise man, honest as well, two qualities rarely found among public officials. He was not one to put on airs, though there were many holding a job like his who became puffed up with their own importance, acting as though they had permission from heaven to order people about.

On the day he arrived at Ye, he came without fanfare. As soon as he settled in, he made a sincere effort to acquaint himself with the villagers and to learn of their needs. Daily he took long walks, nodding now to a man carrying a heavy sack of grain on his back, now to an old grandfather sitting near a wall in the noonday sun. With a polite bow he greeted women threshing wheat and chatted with young boys playing a game of tag. Wandering up one lane and down another, he took notice of every-thing. Most of the dwellings looked as if they would fall apart if struck by a gust of wind. On a dusty road he stepped aside to let a cart pass, and was moved to pity by the condition of the sickly mule pulling it. Syimen Bau could count every one of its protrud-ing ribs. At the edge of the village he saw a man hitched to a plow, barely able to drag himself from one end of the field to the other. Clearly, the people of Ye were wretchedly poor.

During one of his strolls Syimen Bau reached the end of a dirty alleyway. Just beyond it he saw several large houses whose bright tile roofs and heavy carved doors reflected the wealth of their owners. He soon learned that these elaborate homes belonged to the Magistrate, to the Officer in Charge of Ceremonies, and to other village officials. Syimen Bau made a mental note to find out why a few individuals enjoyed great riches while so many others were trapped in hopeless poverty.

After he had been at his post for several weeks, Syimen Bau sent word to the village elders, bidding them to come to his house. When they arrived he made them feel welcome. These wise older men had the respect of their neighbors. Their advice was often sought by the villagers, and it was they who acted as spokesmen in dealings with the officials.

While they were drinking the piping hot tea that a servant had set before them, Syimen Bau said, "I would like to help the people of Ye. I can see, even in the short time that I have been here, that life is not easy for them. If you can tell me what you think is their most serious problem, we could work together to solve it."

The village elders looked from one to the other. No other district prefect had ever talked to them in this kind way or had asked for their counsel. Rising slowly from his seat, one of the elders offered his opinion.

"Honorable Prefect, you speak the truth when you say that life in our village is very hard. It has been so in my memory, in the memory of my father and my grandfather as well. It is not that we do not toil with all our might. You will not find a lazy one among us. But no matter how hard we work, we are bowed down by grinding poverty. It is as though we were doomed forever to carry a mountain on our backs.''

Syimen Bau thanked the man for his reply. Turning to another elder he asked, ''Can you explain to me why this is so? If people are willing to work hard, they may not have many luxuries, but they should at least be able to put a little steamed bread and a few vegetables on their tables every day.''

The second elder bowed respectfully. He hesitated, uncertain of how to answer. ''We are poor because each year we must find a wife for the River God.''

''Indeed,'' replied Syimen Bau. ''And why must you find a wife for the River God?'' He gave not the least sign that the elder's answer had taken him by surprise.

Now the third elder rose to his feet. ''Honorable Sir, the people of our village have always obeyed the laws of the government and the rules of our village officers. Even if they are ordered to do something that causes them great hardship, they never protest.''

With kind encouragement, Syimen Bau urged the elder to proceed.

''Each year the Officer in Charge of Ceremonies and the Magistrate levy crushing taxes on the people of the village. They use two or three hundred thousand cash as expenses for securing a wife for the River God. The rest of the money they share with the village sorceress.'' The other elders shook their heads sadly as if to agree that they all suffered alike from this crushing burden.

''Who is this village sorceress?'' Syimen Bau asked.

''She is an ugly witch,'' explained the elder, ''who for many years has been arranging marriages with the River God. People fear her, yet they often seek her help because they believe she can communicate with the dead and foretell future events. For her services, she is paid handsomely. Even the poorest among us will press their last coins into her hand if she promises to bring back a message from the grave of a revered relative.''

"Where does the sorceress live?" asked Syimen Bau, his suspicions of wrongdoing aroused.

"She lives in a house of many rooms close by the cemetery. It is whispered about," added the elder as if sharing a deep secret, "that she walks among the tombs at night." The old man shuddered.

"If she lives alone, why does she have a house of many rooms?"

"But, Honorable Sir, she does not live alone. She lives with ten disciples whom she trains in the black art of the occult."

"What a strange tale I am being told," thought Syimen Bau, listening even more intently. "Now you must explain to me," he said to the elder, "exactly how the sorceress finds a wife for the River God."

"Since she is acquainted with most of the families in the village, she knows which families have young, pretty daughters. Each year she chooses one family, goes to their house and tells the parents that their daughter has been given the honor of becoming the wife of the River God. She leaves several gifts and takes the girl with her, allowing only a few minutes for tearful farewells. During the next two weeks the chosen bride lives in a special tent which is put up near the river. She is waited on by the old sorceress and her disciples. They bathe her in perfumed water, dress her in new silk gowns, decorate her hair with pearl ornaments. She is given the best food to eat and the choicest wines to drink. She is treated in the manner befitting a royal princess."

"What happens after two weeks?" Syimen Bau pressed the elder to move along more quickly with his narration.

"On the wedding day the bridal bed is made ready. A soft mattress stuffed with a filling of dry straw is covered with beautiful brocade. The sheets are embroidered with silk flowers, the coverlet worthy of the bed of an empress."

"Ah, yes," said Syimen Bau. "Please go on."

"The young girl is washed from head to toe, her skin rubbed with sweet-smelling herbs. Splendidly arrayed in a wedding dress that is the envy of every maiden in the village, she is made to sit on the bridal bed. She is now ready to meet her groom."

"Is that all?" inquired Syimen Bau. The elder had been talking for a long time, and Syimen Bau was growing impatient to get to the end of the story.

"No, Your Honor. The bed is brought to the water's edge and pushed into the river. Carried away by the current, it sinks to the bottom a few miles downstream. The young bride joins her husband, the River God."

Syimen Bau paced the floor. Stopping to face the elders once again, he said, "I do not understand. Why does the River God need a new bride each year?"

It was the first elder's turn to talk. He looked frightened, and his voice quavered. "Your Honor, the sorceress tells us that unless we find a wife for the River God each year, the river will rise and flood our land, and many people will drown. We live in constant fear for our lives. To make matters worse, families with young daughters have been leaving our village in large numbers. There are so few of us left. It becomes harder and harder to find a suitable wife for the River God."

"This is indeed a grave problem," agreed Syimen Bau, "and you may be sure that I shall give it much thought. And now, worthy gentlemen, I bid you good day."

The elders expressed their thanks and started to leave. As they were about to go out the door, Syimen Bau remarked casually, "When the time comes for the next wedding of the River God, be kind enough to invite me. I would very much like to attend the ceremony."

In the early spring a messenger was sent to Syimen Bau to tell him that a young wife had been selected for the River God and that the time for the wedding had been set. When the day arrived,

"Families with young daughters have been leaving our village."

Syimen Bau walked down toward the river. There was still a slight chill in the air, a reminder that winter had ended only a short time ago. About three hundred villagers had gathered along the banks to watch the ceremony. They stood huddled in their padded jackets, talking quietly among themselves. Off to one side stood the sorceress and her disciples. They were clothed in their best dresses, for they considered themselves members of the wedding party.

The Officer in Charge of Ceremonies stepped forth to announce in a loud pompous voice that the ceremony was about to begin. The murmuring ceased and a stillness settled over the crowd. The sorceress and her disciples entered the tent. To the sound of blaring horns the tent flaps parted, and they stepped out, carrying aloft the young maiden bound for her watery abode. Just as the sorceress gave the signal to send the bride on her journey, Syimen Bau called out, "One moment!" All eyes turned toward him. "I want to look at the girl carefully to judge for myself whether she is pretty enough to be the wife of the River God." He walked around her three times, examining her with mock seriousness. "She won't do," he declared. "Positively not!"

"I will tell you what we can do," said Syimen Bau. "We will ask the sorceress to report to the River God. She will tell him that the girl who was selected is not worthy of being his wife, and she will assure His Highness that a search will be undertaken anew. As soon as we can find a beauty who is certain to please him, she will be sent without delay." Before she could make any protest, Syimen Bau ordered two of his strong servants to toss the sorceress into the water.

After a brief interval, noting that the sorceress had failed to return, Syimen Bau asked loudly enough for all to hear, "Why is she tarrying so long? Perhaps we should send someone to find out." He motioned to his servants to grab one of the disciples. As they heaved her into the river, Syimen Bau raised his voice and warned sternly, "Hurry back with your mistress because the people cannot be kept waiting all day."

Syimen Bau allowed a little time to elapse before addressing the crowd. He pretended to be very annoyed. "I can't imagine what could be taking that disciple so long. She is certainly not following my orders. Let us send another one to remind her and her mistress that our patience is wearing thin."

With an almost imperceptible nod of his head he signaled his servants. They dragged a second disciple toward the river. She protested loudly and struggled to free herself, while Syimen Bau admonished, "Tell your mistress that we will deal severely with those who do not follow orders. We insist that she return at once."

When the second disciple also failed to reappear, Syimen Bau spoke to the village officials.

"Well, I should have known better than to send women to talk to the River God. You can see how few brains they have. They cannot even carry out so simple a task as delivering a message and returning with an answer. If you want something done properly, you have to send a man. Surely, the Officer in Charge of Ceremonies can do a better job." Without a second's hesitation, the servants stepped forward, one grabbing the startled victim by his shoulders, the other by his legs, and they swung him out into the deepest part of the river.

Syimen Bau stood silently, peering into the distance. His back was turned to the villagers, and he could hear their nervous whispers. When their restlessness increased, he offered a new proposal.

"Neither the sorceress, nor the disciples, nor the Officer in Charge of Ceremonies has come back. If we next send the Magistrate, a man of his dignity and stature will undoubtedly be able to persuade all the others to return."

An anguished cry rose from the Magistrate's throat. He and all

Syimen Bau ordered his servants to toss the sorceress into the river.

the village officials began to kowtow and beat their heads on the ground.

"Please, Your Honor," they begged, "we have already sent enough messengers."

"Well," offered Syimen Bau, "perhaps you are right. It does seem that the River God has decided to detain his guests for a long time. We may as well return to our homes."

From that day on, nobody in the village of Ye ever again mentioned finding a wife for the River God.

Syimen Bau understood that unless he could devise a way to prevent the recurring floods, the people would once again resort to sorcery. He made plans for an extensive public project. All able-bodied men and boys were conscripted to dig twelve canals, which would lead the water from the river to irrigate the fields. Digging the canals and lining the sides with rocks was back-breaking work, and no one was paid for his labor.

There was plenty of sulking and complaining among the villagers, but the work went forward. Syimen Bau understood that he was not very popular.

"They curse me now," he thought, "but some day I will have their blessing."

After the canals were finished, the threat of flood ceased. The fields have an abundance of water to grow wheat and millet. All who live in the village of Ye have enough to eat and want for nothing. Those who once cursed Syimen Bau have long since joined their ancestors. Today he is revered as a great benefactor, for he gave the villagers the gift of life.

The
White
Snake

High on a craggy mountain veiled in wisps of trailing clouds there once lived a white snake. Her long, graceful body wore a million scales that sparkled and gleamed like precious pearls. Coiled on a warm rocky ledge, basking contentedly in the sunlight, she was often joined by a smaller companion whose skin was greener than the emerald fields of spring.

Both snakes had been living on the mountain from time beyond memory. They paced their daily lives in accordance with the rising and setting of the sun, the waxing and waning of the moon, and the orderly changing of the seasons. Never once had they violated a single natural law. Because their communion with nature was so perfect, they had acquired the power to transform themselves into humans.

One balmy spring morning the green snake was feeling unusually restless. "It is dull lying here on the ledge day after day," she remarked. "Wouldn't it be fun to have an adventure once in a while?"

"What do you have in mind?" asked the white snake, suspecting that her friend would suggest chasing rabbits through the grass.

"Well," answered the green snake cautiously, "I have been thinking for some time how exciting it would be to leave the mountain."

"And where would we go?" the white snake inquired, lifting her head.

Her companion pressed on. "For a long time I have wanted to visit the city of Hangchow."

"That would be a foolish thing to do," cautioned the white snake. "Whatever would snakes do in a city?"

"Oh, no, not as snakes." Mischief twinkled in the green snake's eyes. "Remember, we have the power to transform ourselves. You could go as a beautiful young lady, and I," she concluded, her voice rising with excitement, "shall go as your maidservant."

The white snake was sure that the whole idea was harebrained, even dangerous. She declared she would have nothing to do with such a silly escapade.

But the green snake persisted. "Please," she begged, "let us try it just once. If it proves to be troublesome, we can simply return to the mountain."

The white snake felt uneasy as she silently imagined the many pitfalls they might encounter. In the end she gave in, because she loved her friend dearly and did not wish to dampen her spirits.

The ancients tell how the two snakes changed themselves into human forms. First they uncoiled to their full length, stretching their heads upward. Then, starting from the topmost point, their skins began to crack open and slowly peel away. Emerging as if from a cocoon, appeared the heads of two maidens. Their bodies were in exquisite proportion from their gently sloping shoulders to their delicately shaped legs. Once the last of their snakeskins dropped to the ground, they were beautiful to behold.

By some magic which mortals cannot explain, only a fraction of a moment passed before they were fully clothed. One was adorned in a shimmering white gown embroidered with gold thread. "From now on I shall be called Pure Virtue," she announced. Her friend, wearing a dainty green blouse over a flowing skirt, chose the name Little Green. Soft, satin slippers hugging their feet comfortably, they took their first steps, heads held high, hips swaying gently.

The two maidens enjoyed ambling along the winding path that led down the mountain. The air was warm and a faint breeze shook the tree branches laden with fragrant blossoms. The azure sky held not a single cloud. All was serene except for the occasional singing of a cricket or the shrill call of a bird.

After they had walked a while, the terrain changed. The path narrowed and became rough and slippery underfoot. When it wound about the edge of a precipice, they were terrified. The slightest misstep would have meant a plunge to the bottom of the chasm and certain death. As snakes, they could easily have crawled among the overhanging cliffs, but as humans they quaked with fear. Not until they reached level ground did they feel a sense of relief.

By the time they neared the outskirts of Hangchow, they were walking on a busy road. Carts pulled by long-horned oxen and filled to overflowing with grain rumbled toward the market square. Men and women, carrying baskets of fruits and vegetables, hurried in the same direction. Pure Virtue and Little Green joined the throng, and by midday found themselves in the center of the city.

Both sides of the narrow, bustling streets were lined with small shops. The curious maidens stopped frequently to admire displays of intricately carved jade and gold jewelry. Hung from outdoor stalls was an unending assortment of the finest textured silks in every imaginable design and color. Trays of scented herbs and sacks of green tea gave off a pungent aroma. Thrilled with the sights and sounds of the marketplace, they walked on.

When they reached West Lake they gasped with pleasure. Tall, slender-leafed willow trees lined the shore. The surface of the lake was dotted with flat-bottomed boats fitted with red and white canopies. Where the water was deepest, a few larger craft were being poled noiselessly along by broad-shouldered ferrymen. Overhead, long-tailed kites wafted lazily in the air, their taut strings held fast by delighted children. Someone could be heard singing a lilting melody to the accompaniment of a stringed instrument. Leading from the shore out over the water stretched a zigzag walkway crowded with strollers admiring the schools of golden carp. Pure Virtue and Little Green were thrilled with each new sight and sound.

In a clearing close to the water's edge they spied a weathered boathouse. Near it, a man wearing a cone-shaped hat to shade his face called to the passersby.

"Come take a ride in my boat. The weather is fine, the water is smooth, the price is cheap." He kept repeating the same sing-song cry, stopping only now and then to collect a fare from a customer. "Only room for two more. The weather is fine, the water is smooth, the price is cheap."

Pure Virtue and Little Green approached the boathouse, their eyes sparkling in anticipation of a new adventure. They quickly paid the fare, got on board, and were led to the two remaining empty seats.

Then, trousers rolled up to his knees, the nimble boatman jumped over the side, waded through the shallow water, and untied the holding rope from around the stump of a tree. With little effort, he climbed back in, picked up a long pole, and started to ease the boat away from the shore. Soon the craft was gliding smoothly through the water.

A dozen seats were arranged along the sides of the boat. In the center stood a small but sturdy table where watermelon seeds and peanuts had been set out for the enjoyment of the passengers. Seated next to Pure Virtue was a well-dressed, handsome young man holding an umbrella on his lap. The two kept glancing shyly at each other, but neither could summon up the courage to start a conversation.

"Look to your right," shouted the boatman. Looming ahead was a group of three rocks. "On a bright night," he explained, "when the moonlight strikes the rocks, three shimmering orbs may be seen floating on the water. It is a sight you should not miss. Ride with me of an evening," he urged, "and I will show you this marvel of nature."

As if by prior arrangement, Pure Virtue and the young man exclaimed in unison, "How wonderful!" They looked at each other and smiled. Politely, the young man introduced himself.

"I am Syu Syan," he offered. "I was born into a poor but respected family. When my parents died I came to Hangchow to live with my older sister. I have found employment in an apothecary shop where I sell herbs." Expectantly, he awaited a response from the attractive young girl at his side.

"I am called Pure Virtue, and this is my maidservant, Little Green. We have only recently arrived in the neighborhood."

Soon they were chattering like old friends. The conversation went from one topic to another. Pure Virtue and Syu Syan barely heard what was going on around them. When the boatman called out that they were nearing the end of the ride, they looked up in surprise.

The spring weather in this part of China has always been unpredictable. One minute the sun casts its warm rays over hills and fields. The next moment ominous, dark clouds gather, sending man and beast fleeing for shelter. When people venture out of their homes, they often carry umbrellas in the event of a sudden downpour.

No sooner had the boatman tied the ropes securely to the tree stump when the sky became overcast. "A stroke of good luck," Syu Syan thought to himself. "Fate has intervened. I shall be able to see Pure Virtue again."

"Please," he offered, "take my umbrella. You will be drenched by the time you return to your lodging."

"That is very kind of you," said Pure Virtue, "but when will we be able to return it?"

"Tomorrow is time enough," Syu Syan replied.

"Please, take my umbrella," offered Syu Syan.

"If you will tell us where you live, my maid will deliver the umbrella to your house in the early morning," Pure Virtue promised.

Syu Syan gave very careful directions to Pure Virtue and Little Green. Then, bowing from the waist, he wished them a good afternoon and left.

On the following day, Little Green arrived at Syu Syan's door. Along with his umbrella she brought a note from Pure Virtue in which she thanked him for his kindness and expressed the hope that they would meet again soon. Syu Syan was delighted. He had fallen in love with Pure Virtue from the moment he had seen her board the boat.

Pure Virtue and Little Green frequently took walks around West Lake, and, by arrangement, Syu Syan was always there to meet them. From day to day their affection for one another grew stronger. No longer able to hide her feelings, Pure Virtue confessed to Little Green that she was in love, and wanted, more than anything else, to marry Syu Syan.

"Please do not forget that you are, after all, a snake," Little Green begged her mistress. "To pretend that it is your real nature to walk erect upon two feet instead of crawling on your belly is tempting fate. I warn you, our secret is bound to be discovered, and when the truth is revealed, we shall all suffer a terrible end."

But you might as well reason with a river in flood as with a young girl in love.

"Have no fear," Pure Virtue assured her. "I will be very careful never to reveal our true nature. My only wish is to be a good wife to Syu Syan. Already my head is full of wonderful plans for the future. And you, my dearest friend," she said to Little Green, "will live with us as one of the family."

A short time after the wedding, Pure Virtue suggested to her husband that they turn the front room of their house into a chemist's shop. "We live on a busy street," she told him, "and I am certain we will not lack for customers. Of this you can be sure, people are always getting sick and needing remedies. With my knowledge of herbal medicine,'' she continued, ''it would not be hard for me to teach you how to mix the herbs and prepare prescriptions.''

Syu Syan eagerly agreed. To be a respectable shop owner was far better than being at the mercy of a grouchy employer who demanded long hours of work for a few miserable coins.

Pure Virtue was a wonderful teacher and Syu Syan an equally good student. Within a short time, he became a skilled dispenser of healing potions. As his reputation grew, so did the money jingling in his pockets.

The sages caution that the greatest happiness is often stalked by sorrow impatient to take its place.

A distance from the city of Hangchow, carved into a bluff rising steeply above the sea, stood the Golden Mountain Temple. Here, saffron-robed monks chanted their daily prayers in search of inner harmony. At the sound of the deep-toned gong, they filed out in orderly procession to take up their daily tasks.

Among them lived Fa Hai, a monk renowned for his power to ferret out evil wherever it might appear. One crisp, autumn day, while traveling through the city of Hangchow, he noticed a black cloud hanging motionless over the roof of a small apothecary shop.

''How unusual,'' he mumbled, studying an otherwise perfectly clear sky. ''A cloud such as this is a sinister sign.''

Peering into the shop, he saw Syu Syan sitting behind the counter, entering the morning's sales in his record book. Fa Hai caught his eye and motioned to him to step outside.

''Young man,'' he confided in a guarded whisper, ''I sense some evil lurking nearby. The black cloud that sits in the heavens above your house is a sign of bad luck. Have you any reason to suspect there may be a spirit living with you?''

''Impossible,'' said Syu Syan, quite annoyed, although he did not wish to seem disrespectful to a holy man. ''There are only three people residing in my house."

"Then tell me who they are," insisted the monk.

"My wife, her maid, and I," replied Syu Syan.

"I am almost certain," Fa Hai said, sadly shaking his head from side to side, "that it is your wife who harbors some demon spirit within her."

Syu Syan stared aghast at this stranger who had appeared from nowhere to shatter his peaceful life. He could only repeat meekly, "I do not believe what you say. This must be some dreadful mistake."

"I see that you still doubt the truth of what I tell you," Fa Hai persisted. He took a step closer to Syu Syan, keeping his voice low so as not to be overheard.

"Very well, my good man," he warned. "But I must tell you again that if you do not get rid of your wife, she will bring a curse upon your house and all who live in it. I will prove to you that I know whereof I speak." He reached into his wide sleeve and withdrew a little packet. "Here," he urged, "take it," and he placed it into Syu Syan's hand. "It contains a special potion. Add it to a glass of wine and ask your wife to drink it." Without another word, the monk turned and hurried off.

Syu Syan tried not to betray the fear that gripped his heart. Neither Pure Virtue nor Little Green suspected anything out of the ordinary, for he went about his work as usual. At times he almost succeeded in convincing himself that the monk was just an imposter bent on stirring up trouble. But each time he determined to put the whole thing out of his mind, it came back to nag him with disturbing doubt.

The second day after Fa Hai's visit was the time of the Dragon Boat Festival. It was the custom, as part of the celebration, to drink a bit of wine made with the rare herb realgar. A taste of this wine, taken on the festival day, would guarantee good health during the hot summer months.

While Pure Virtue busied herself about the stove preparing the

Syu Syan lost consciousness and collapsed on the floor.

midday meal, Syu Syan opened the monk's paper packet, slipped a few grains of the potion into a cup, and filled it with wine. "Come, let us celebrate in honor of the Dragon Boat Festival," he said to Pure Virtue, attempting to sound cheerful. "We will drink to our good health."

"Please, not now," pleaded Pure Virtue. "Wine does not agree with me, especially before a meal."

"Just a sip or two can't hurt," he coaxed, handing her the cup. Syu Syan emptied his drink in one gulp, then motioned to Pure Virtue to do the same. It was not in her nature to displease her husband, and she did not resist his urging.

As soon as she swallowed the last drop, her head began to spin. She told Syu Syan that she felt dizzy and wanted to lie down for a short nap. "Please eat without me," she begged. "I will not sleep very long."

Syu Syan finished his bowl of noodles. Without making a sound, he entered the bedchamber to see if Pure Virtue was still asleep. Ever so gently he lifted the mosquito netting. Terror seized him. His face turned ghostly white. There, instead of Pure Virtue, a long white snake lay coiled on the bed. In a state of shock, Syu Syan lost consciousness and collapsed on the floor.

A little while later the effects of the wine wore off, and Pure Virtue awoke to find Syu Syan lying lifeless beside the bed. When she failed to rouse him, she shouted for Little Green to come and help. But no matter how hard they tried, they could not revive him.

Little Green wanted to comfort her mistress, who was weeping inconsolably. "Do not despair," she said, bending over Syu Syan and bringing her ear close to his chest. "Just as I thought," she declared, "Syu Syan is not dead. He is in a deep coma, but he is breathing. There is still hope."

Little Green put her arms around Pure Virtue and spoke to her calmly. "Think hard, there must be a cure. You are so wise in the art of herbal medicine. Surely there is something that will restore Syu Syan.''

Suddenly Pure Virtue freed herself from Little Green's embrace.

"What is it?'' asked Little Green.

"Of course, the ling-jr herb from the Fairy Mountain.'' There was a note of regained confidence in Pure Virtue's voice. "Nothing else will work.''

"Oh, how impossible you are,'' said Little Green. "Do you not know that the ling-jr herb is so rare and precious it is guarded night and day by fierce guards of the Fairy Queen?''

"No matter. Whatever the obstacles, I will overcome them.'' Pure Virtue had already decided what she must do, and she would not listen to any warnings of danger.

To reach the Fairy Queen's palace, Pure Virtue had to climb a mountain strewn with sharp rocks. Thorny brambles tore at her clothes and scratched her legs. By the time she arrived, she was bleeding and exhausted. Her clothes were ripped, her hair full of burrs.

The deer fairy and the crane fairy, who stood guard at the palace gate, would not let her pass. But she was on a desperate mission, and when they refused to listen to her entreaties, she started to beat them with her bare hands. The guards seized her, pinning her against the palace wall while they sent a messenger to tell the Fairy Queen about the rude and stubborn prisoner. The Queen ordered that Pure Virtue be brought before her at once.

"Can you explain your unspeakable behavior?'' demanded the Queen, glaring at Pure Virtue. Pure Virtue bowed deeply to show proper humility and addressed the Queen meekly.

"Your Majesty, do not judge me to be unruly or discourteous. My dear husband lies near death. He can be cured only by the ling-jr herb that you alone possess. I beg you to give me just one small dose that I may save his life.''

The Fairy Queen, though she remained stern and unsmiling,

was not without compassion. She was touched by Pure Virtue's grief, but there was a more subtle reason for her pity. Endowed with the power to see into the future, she knew that a son would be born to Pure Virtue whose destiny it was to become an important officer of the royal court. The Fairy Queen made her decision.

"Though you behaved poorly," she said, "I can understand the deep love you bear for your husband. For such great devotion and courage you deserve praise. Your wish shall be granted."

Clutching the precious herb in her hand, Pure Virtue hurried home. As if by a miracle, Syu Syan was soon back on his feet, but most of the time he seemed downcast and ill at ease. He never mentioned the incident in the bedchamber, though it had left its mark. He kept to himself, rarely speaking to a soul in the house or in the shop. Nothing seemed to give him any pleasure, not the delicious food Pure Virtue prepared for him, not the company of his friends, not even his growing prosperity.

It was only after Pure Virtue had given birth to a healthy son that his mood improved. To have a first-born male child was seen as a special gift bestowed by heaven. The proud parents called him Shr-lin and rejoiced at their good fortune. Little Green forgot her former fears sharing in their happiness.

It was not long after the birth of the child that Fa Hai returned to the city for a second time. When he appeared at the door of the shop, Syu Syan was alone. Without so much as a customary bow, the monk began his direful warning.

"I have come to tell you for the last time that the black cloud still casts its shadow upon your house. As long as you live under the same roof with your wife you will not be able to escape calamity. Better to join me and live among the holy monks in the Golden Mountain Temple. In our company you will lead a simple life, seeking neither wealth nor fame. There we will pray and fast together, and you will find peace. Remain here, and to the end of your days misery will dog your every step."

Syu Syan started to tremble. The image of the white snake

lying on his bed reawakened fears he had tried to suppress. "I will go with you," he said humbly. Without a word to anyone, he left the shop and followed the old monk.

Pure Virtue was sorely perplexed by Syu Syan's disappearance, until she learned that the monk had lured her husband away. Furious, she vowed to bring him back. Fa Hai was just as determined to save Syu Syan from her sorcery. When Pure Virtue arrived at the temple and demanded that her husband be released at once, Fa Hai scorned her pleas. He told her that she was unworthy to be the wife of such a good man. This only infuriated Pure Virtue further. It was time to punish this insolent monk with a few of her own magic tricks.

During her former life she had made many friends among the crawly, slippery creatures that dwell in the depths of the ocean. She now commanded them to raise the winds and roil the waters, causing the surging sea to flood the temple. The shrimp, the crabs, and all the fish, both great and small, tried with all their might to obey. Churning up wild foamy sprays, they sent waves crashing against the mountain. Pure Virtue goaded them on to greater effort. The waters rose, fell, spun around in wild eddies. Through it all the mighty mountain withstood the onslaught, and the temple, on its lofty peak, remained firm and dry.

Pure Virtue realized she was in grave danger and would have to flee for her life. Dashing across the temple grounds toward the stone steps that would lead her down the mountain, she caught sight of Syu Syan. She ran toward him, risking capture, and implored him to return home.

"This cunning monk has bewitched you and destroyed our happy life," she sobbed. "What could he have told you to make you leave me?"

Syu Syan did not reply. He just stood there, mute and uncomfortable. Her words passed over his head, and were carried away by the wind. When he turned his back to her she knew she had lost him forever.

Fa Hai caught up with Pure Virtue. His face was convulsed with rage. From within the folds of his robe, he withdrew a lacquered box and began to recite a magic incantation. Pure Virtue was transfixed under his spell, her feet glued to the ground. In an instant, her skin was covered over by a sheath of white scales. She was no longer human. With great effort Fa Hai squeezed and pushed a writhing, squirming snake into his box. He slammed down the cover.

Satisfied that he had vanquished evil, Fa Hai handed the box to his disciples and directed them to take it back to the city of Hangchow. There, in a black hole beneath the Leifeng Pagoda, the white snake was imprisoned for life.

"You may return home," Fa Hai told Syu Syan. "Your wife will no longer trouble you."

When Syu Syan entered his house, all was still. His son was asleep in his bed, but Little Green was nowhere to be found. Syu Syan never saw her again.

Through the ensuing years, Syu Syan raised his son with great tenderness, taking on the duties of both mother and father. When the boy was old enough for schooling, he hired the best of tutors, sparing no expense. Later he encouraged him to prepare for the difficult civil service examinations. How proud he was to learn that his son had passed the tests with the highest grades in all of China! Shortly thereafter, Shr-lin was appointed to an important position at the royal court. The Fairy Queen's prediction had come true.

The relentless passage of time turned Syu Syan's hair gray. He often wandered back to thoughts of Pure Virtue and the love they had shared.

"Your mother was a good and virtuous woman, always devoted to her family," he would tell Shr-lin. "People admired her for her skill in herbal healing, and blessed her when she helped them recover their health. Surely she did not deserve the fate that befell her."

Every year, father and son visit the Leifeng Pagoda. There they pray that Pure Virtue's soul will be granted a permanent resting place in heaven, and that she will reside forever among the Immortals.

The
Golden
Carp

At the foot of a soaring mountain, there once lived a tribe of people whose chieftain was known as Cave Lord Wu. He was called by this name for he had chosen to make a home for his two wives within the rocky vastness of a large, high-domed cave.

It was Wu's misfortune that his first wife died shortly after giving birth to a baby girl. From an early age it was evident that the girl, named Ye Syan, was endowed with grace and charm. Gentle of nature and kind of heart, she was dearly loved by her father who saw in her all the admirable qualities of his departed wife.

Destiny did not decree that Wu have a long life. Well before Ye Syan reached marriageable age, he sickened and lapsed into a lethargy from which he could not be roused. All the healing herbs gave him little relief, and all the sacrifices offered to bring about his recovery were useless. Within a week of the onset of his illness, he was dead, leaving Ye Syan in the care of his second wife.

Now that Wu was gone, Ye Syan was at the mercy of her stepmother, a mean, jealous woman. She had long resented Wu's favoritism toward Ye Syan while he ignored her own daughter, an unattractive, dull girl. Wu's death left the stepmother free to take out her bitterness by mistreating Ye Syan without fear of interference from anyone.

Her own daughter was given easy tasks to perform and kept close to home, while Ye Syan was assigned the most unpleasant, arduous chores. Daily, in fair weather or foul, the stepmother would send her out to gather firewood in the higher mountain forests or to lug back buckets of drinking water from distant streams.

On one such errand, Ye Syan happened upon a lake fed by underground springs. As she was about to dip her bucket into the mirror-clear water, she was attracted by a sudden flash of color. It was a tiny fish, no longer than her pinky. Scooping it up, she watched with fascination as it swam round and round inside one of her wooden buckets. How she longed to take it home! The little fish would be a friend when she was lonely, and a comfort when she was abused. Her stepmother was sure to disapprove, but Ye Syan decided there and then to keep it as a pet. She hitched the two buckets full of water to her carrying pole. Unmindful of the heavy weight across her back, half walking, half running, she managed to arrive home without spilling a drop.

Before entering the cave, she transferred her precious fish to an old basin, and thereafter kept it hidden, tucked out of sight. Each day she secretly fed it a few grains of rice from her own bowl, and each day she saw it become longer and more beautiful.

With bright orange fins and a lacy fantail, it soon outgrew the basin, and Ye Syan realized that her fish needed more space. Taking care not to be seen by her stepmother, she was able to carry it, undetected, out of the cave. She took it to a nearby pond, where, within a short time, it reached full size.

Whenever Ye Syan came to the pond, her wonderful fish would surface and flash its fiery fins as if to greet her. Then it would twist sideways, jump straight up into the air, and splash back into the water. As long as she remained there, it entertained her with its playful antics.

The stepmother's curiosity was aroused when she noticed that Ye Syan was spending a great deal of time near the pond. "That lazy wastrel of a girl, idling away hours better given to useful work," she complained. "I'll soon find out what she is up to."

When Ye Syan left the cave that evening, her stepmother followed her. Hidden behind a scraggly bush, she witnessed a strange spectacle. As Ye Syan neared the edge of the pond, a brilliant orange fish with glassy, bulging eyes emerged from the water. It rested its scaly head on the gravel bank and permitted Ye Syan to stroke it. With a wave of its lacy tail, it turned and plopped back into the pool.

"So that is how she spends her time, in useless play with a fish!" the stepmother fumed. "This I will not tolerate! Besides, that fish will make a delicious meal. I must have it."

Several times thereafter the determined woman came to the pond and waited patiently, but in vain. The fish never showed itself. Disappointed, she would leave empty-handed to return again and again for naught. During the ensuing days she could think of nothing else but how to catch the fish.

Ye Syan came home later than usual one day, tired and footsore, having carried a heavy load of kindling from a far-off woodland. She steeled herself against the usual scolding she expected. Instead, her stepmother greeted her with disarming kindness.

"You dear girl, how hard you have been working," she cooed. "Because you are not lazy and do your chores without complaining, you deserve a reward. See, I have made you a new blouse. Do try it on and give me the old one you are wearing. I shall put it in the rag pile, for it is too shabby to be worth mending."

Ye Syan did not comprehend the change in her stepmother's attitude. Nevertheless, she accepted her offer with a great sense of relief. "Perhaps," she dared to hope, "my life will not be so hard from now on."

The blouse, with its embroidered neck and narrow sleeves, was very becoming. Ye Syan was happier than she had been in all the time since her father's death.

The following morning she was sent off as usual to fetch the day's supply of drinking water.

Her wonderful fish would surface and flash its fiery fins.

"I have learned of a spring that has the sweetest and clearest water to be found anywhere," explained her stepmother. "To reach it you must follow the path that winds to the top of the mountain. It is a long distance to go, and you may need to rest along the way. Do not worry if you return later than usual. I shall keep your supper warm."

Within moments after Ye Syan left the cave the scheming stepmother changed into Ye Syan's old clothes, concealing a knife in her waistband. So anxious was she to reach the pond, she almost tripped in her haste to get there. Out of breath, she sat down at the water's edge, when, to her amazement, the fish appeared at her feet. Quick as lightning she pulled it from the water, lopped off its head, and carried it back to her cave home. A pot of simmering fish broth soon filled the air with a delicious aroma. The stepmother and her daughter feasted on the tasty fish to the last savory morsel.

"I shall bury the fishbones in the dunghill," the stepmother said to her daughter. "No one will ever find them there."

Tired from her unusually long walk, Ye Syan returned to find only a bowl of cold rice for her evening meal. Her stepmother spoke not a word, and her stepsister sat fidgeting with her fingers. Ye Syan ate in silence, washed the rice bowl, and, as was her custom, rushed to the pond to visit with her pet. For the first time ever, the fish failed to greet her. Though she called to it repeatedly, the water's surface remained unruffled. She scanned every inch of the pond till her eyes ached. That evening and the next and the next, Ye Syan came to the pond, praying that her fish would return. Each time, she threw grains of rice into the water to tempt it with food, but her friend did not appear. At last, overwhelmed with a sense of loss, she burst into tears. For a long time, she sat near the pond, sick at heart and weeping.

By this time it had turned quite dark. Ye Syan stood up and brushed the soil from her clothes. She had not noticed the bent old stranger leaning on a cane, watching her from the shadows.

"Dry your tears, my child," he said. "The evil deed is done. The fish was killed by your stepmother. You will find its bones in the dunghill. Dig them out and keep them always. Wherever fortune may lead, they will serve you well."

Before Ye Syan could open her lips to reply, the stranger was gone.

The day of a great festival was at hand. In cave homes tunneled into the hillsides and in huts that dotted the valleys, people prepared for the celebration. They looked forward to seeing richly costumed dancers perform to the beat of drums and the clash of cymbals. They would watch acrobats and mummers entertain with acts of daring and pantomime. All manner of delicacies would be offered to please the eye and tempt the appetite. It was the one time in the entire year when people could cease their daily labors and lose themselves in the gaiety of the festivities.

"You will remain at home to guard the fruit orchard," Ye Syan's stepmother declared while she and her daughter readied themselves for the grand occasion. On the way out the door, arrayed in their gaudiest dresses, the stepmother hurled a parting warning at Ye Syan. "When we return, if a single piece of fruit is missing, you will pay dearly!"

Ye Syan often brooded over the unfair treatment she suffered at the hands of her stepmother. For the most part she accepted her lot with resignation. Now to be kept from attending the festival was a cruelty hard to bear. Recalling the stranger's talk about the fishbones, she decided to put them to the test, but so great was her gloom she doubted they would be of any help to her.

With great care, Ye Syan took the fishbones from their hiding place. Then, covering her face with her hands, she made a silent wish.

When she opened her eyes, all about her was a soft mist. Suddenly, a beam of intense light pierced the grayness and shone down on her bed. There, neatly laid out, was a skirt of patterned satin, a matching blouse, and a pair of exquisitely embroidered

Ye Syan looked like a goddess!

slippers. Reaching out, she touched them lightly. Yes, they were real! With hesitation, Ye Syan put on the skirt and blouse. The fabric was as soft as gossamer, the colors deep and rich. Then she pulled on the slippers. The transformation was almost miraculous. She looked like a goddess!

A bird released from its cage could not have been happier than Ye Syan as she set off to join the festival celebration. Mingling with the crowds, the extraordinarily beautiful girl became the object of much attention. Along with everyone else, her stepmother and stepsister wondered who she might be.

"Does she not resemble Ye Syan?" the stepsister asked her mother.

"Nonsense," replied the stepmother, dismissing the idea as preposterous. She had told Ye Syan to stay at home and she did not expect to be disobeyed.

Ye Syan joined a ring of spectators that had formed around a group of acrobats. Directly opposite her she spied her stepmother and stepsister. Terrified that they might recognize her, she fled. Frantically pushing her way through the dense crowd of merrymakers, she lost one of her slippers. In her panic, she did not stop to look for it but continued to run, swiftly as a deer, straight toward home.

Upon returning from the festival, the stepmother found Ye Syan asleep in the orchard under a pear tree.

"You see," she said to her daughter, "you were mistaken. The beautiful girl we saw at the festival could not have been Ye Syan."

On the following day, the slipper was found by a poor peasant who sold it for a few coins to an official of the Tuo Huan kingdom.

The Tuo Huan king ruled over a vast territory that included twenty-four islands. Because of his legendary wealth and powerful army, he was envied and feared by all the other weaker tribes. Though he lacked for nothing, he was never content with the riches he had amassed. His craving for more gold, more jewels, even pretty trinkets that caught his fancy, could not be satisfied. The official, anxious to find favor at court, presented the slipper to his king as a gift.

The king was intrigued by the tiny embroidered slipper. "Where is there a maiden," he wondered, "with a foot so dainty? Surely the slipper must belong to a high-born beauty." He resolved to find its owner.

All the young women attached to the palace were required to try on the slipper. Not one of them did it fit. The king then issued a decree that every woman in his kingdom try on his treasured slipper. He sent couriers to every corner of his twenty-four islands, but they all returned without success. Finally, he decided to extend the search beyond his own lands.

The soldier who was dispatched to the area of the cave people never believed he would find the owner of the slipper among its poor inhabitants. When Ye Syan's stepmother led him into her cave dwelling, he was convinced that neither of the two young girls he saw there would be the one he sought. But the king's decree was plain. No one was to be overlooked. The soldier asked Ye Syan's stepsister to try on the slipper first. She tugged and pulled but could not squeeze more than her big toe into it. He handed the slipper to Ye Syan, fully expecting the same results. To the soldier's great surprise, it clung to her foot as though it had been made especially for her.

Still the soldier was unconvinced. It was so unlikely that this ragamuffin would own such a fine slipper. "Give me that slipper," he demanded. "I shall try it on your foot myself." Again, the fit was perfect. Still beset by doubts, he asked Ye Syan if she could produce its mate.

From under her straw mattress Ye Syan drew out the other slipper and stepped into it before her open-mouthed stepmother and stepsister.

"You must come with me to the king's palace," the soldier

said. "My orders are to bring back the maiden whose foot fits the slipper."

Ye Syan asked for time to change her clothes. Quickly, she threw off her old worn rags. She returned wearing her lovely new outfit. The stepmother, astonished by the change in her appearance, recognized that the attractive girl she had seen at the festival was indeed Ye Syan. Her jealousy and wrath knew no bounds, but she could only look on helplessly. Escorted by the king's soldier, Ye Syan went to the palace carrying the magic fishbones with her.

At first sight, the Tuo Huan king was taken with her lovely face and the grace with which she moved in her dainty slippers. He listened courteously while she recounted the story of her golden fish and its cruel end at the hands of her stepmother. Spreading out her fishbones before him, she told of their magic power to grant her wishes.

Unbelieving, the king requested that she demonstrate their power by making a wish for a gold bracelet. In less than a breath, a band of purest gold lay on the table before him. Still unsure, the king asked Ye Syan to wish for a gold ring. In a twinkling, on his third finger appeared a ring encrusted with glittering rubies. The king was jubilant.

"I shall take Ye Syan for my wife, and she will be forever at my side," he announced to his courtiers.

From the day of their marriage, the temptation of the magic fishbones gave the Tuo Huan king no peace. He demanded that Ye Syan ask them for more and more precious gifts to fill the coffers of his island kingdom. Although his wealth increased a hundredfold, his thirst for still greater riches was never slaked.

After a time the bones grew weary of satisfying the greedy ruler's incessant requests. They would give no more. Disgusted with their lack of response, the king ordered Ye Syan to discard them.

But Ye Syan remembered the golden carp that had befriended

her in her loneliest and most desperate hours. She gently placed the bones in a silken pouch and carried them a great distance to a remote spot on the beach. With her own hands she dug a bowl-shaped hole. Wishing each bone a fond farewell, she lowered them into the cool earth. Reverently she marked their burying place with a circle of precious pearls.

The waves that lapped the shore flowed endlessly in and out. The tide rose and ebbed. The water scoured the beach and carried the bones out to sea.

Liang
Shanbo
and
Ju
Yingtai

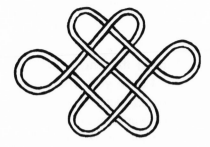

The Ju family was indeed fortunate. Heaven had bestowed upon them the blessing of eight sons and, finally, a daughter. As may be expected, the little girl, Yingtai, was pampered and allowed the privileges of her older brothers. Laughter filled the inner court-yard as she joined in their rough, boyish games. Her parents over-looked her participation in their frequent pranks, for they were pleased that she was in good health and had a happy disposition.

According to custom the sons received their early schooling at home. A tutor who lived with the family instructed his young pupils in the use of brush and ink, and drilled them in the writing of the intricate Chinese characters. In preparation for their formal education they spent long hours each day pouring over books, learning to recite by heart passages from the writings of the great masters. One by one, as Yingtai's brothers grew old enough, they were sent off to school in Hangchow.

By the time Yingtai was thirteen years old, she had lost her playmates, and she was lonely. Sitting at the window embroider-ing a sash with yellow butterflies, she wished that she, too, could join her brothers at school. She remembered how downcast she had felt when the tutor sent her out of the room during the boys' study periods. Sometimes she would stand at the door and listen to them recite their lessons. When no one was looking, she would peek into her brothers' notebooks and secretly copy out pages of characters.

"How unfair!" Yingtai thought, "that I should be treated differently just because I am a girl. There must be some way I, too, can become a scholar." That evening when dinner was almost over and her father was about to leave the table, she found enough courage to make an unusual request.

"Honorable Father," Yingtai began in a low, timid voice, "I would like to ask a special favor."

"My daughter," answered her father tenderly, "if it is at all possible, I shall certainly not deny your request." "Honorable Father," Yingtai began again, "I want to go away to school just as my brothers have done." Afraid that her father would interrupt before she could present her case, she hurried on. "I also long to be a scholar, to study the writings of the sages."

At first, Yingtai's father was amused by his daughter's unexpected wish, then he became serious. "Dear daughter, what you are asking is quite impossible for me to grant. Even if I thought it right for you to be sent off to school, I could not allow it. Only boys may attend school away from home. There is no place for girls, and you would not be accepted. Furthermore, girls are not suited for serious learning, nor is there any need for them to bend over books, for their role in life is to marry and raise children. No, my dear daughter, I cannot even consider such a possibility."

Yingtai choked back her tears and ran from the room. She threw herself on her bed. When she had exhausted all her tears, she fell into a fitful sleep. The next morning she refused to eat or leave her darkened bedchamber. In the days that followed, neither her parents nor the servants could persuade her to take so much as a bowl of broth. The glow in her cheeks faded, the light in her eyes dimmed, her hair became dull and limp.

But her father remained firm. "It is out of the question, she cannot go away to school. She must stay at home as is the custom. Do not concern yourself," he told his wife, "she will come to her senses eventually."

Another long, worrisome week passed, and still Yingtai could not be enticed out of her self-imposed seclusion. Having tried all manner of persuasion and failed, her parents were nearly beside themselves with anxiety. They were gloomily wondering what to do next, when there was a knock at the door.

"The caller is a young doctor," the maid reported. "He wishes to speak to the father of the ailing girl. He claims to have heard about your daughter's illness and is certain that he can restore her to health."

"Show him in," said Yingtai's father. "Perhaps he is the answer to our prayers."

When the doctor stood before the anguished parents, they were somewhat taken aback by his apparent youthfulness, but his deep voice, his dignified dress, and his self-confident manner set them at ease.

"Your daughter is suffering from an ailment not uncommon to girls her age," he said seriously. "It may be fatal if neglected, but treated in time, it can be cured. First, however, you must permit me to examine her."

Yingtai's parents led the doctor to the family's sleeping quarters in the east wing of the house. The maid placed a chair outside Yingtai's bedroom door and bade the doctor be seated.

From his pocket, the doctor produced a long red string. "I must take the girl's pulse. Please tie one end of the string to the patient's left wrist," he directed the maid. "I shall be able to count her heartbeats by holding on to the other end." The maid obeyed.

Brow furrowed as if lost in thought, the doctor remained silent. Each minute seemed an hour as the parents awaited his diagnosis. Finally, the doctor cleared his throat and declared in his best professional manner, "Just as I thought. It is merely a question of securing the right medicine. I shall prescribe a special elixir which contains several rare ingredients. Allow me a few moments to write down the list of items you must purchase at the chemist's shop." He asked for paper, a brush, and ink. Seating himself at a small table, he wrote slowly and with great concentration.

The task finished, he rose and bowed respectfully. "These are the ten things you will need. I shall read them aloud so that you will make no mistakes. If the prescription is not followed to the letter, your daughter will not recover. Please listen closely. You will obtain the following: one measure of dragon horn powder, the brain of a shrimp, dust from a ten-thousand-year-old house, a sprinkling of a thousand-year-old frost, an egg of the bird that dwells in the sun, the intestines of an ant, the ling-jr herb from the Fairy Mountain, the fragrance of the heavenly angels, water from the bottle that belongs to Buddha, and a sample of wine served at the party of the goddesses."

Yingtai's parents were stunned. Her father glared angrily at the doctor, suspecting a hoax. Her mother, equally distrustful, but of a more gentle nature than her husband, asked in a trembling voice, "How can we possibly find these things? Surely you cannot be serious. Are you playing some kind of joke on us?"

"Yes, dear mother, it is a joke," answered Yingtai in her normal tone while pulling off her disguise. "If my own parents cannot recognize me dressed as a young man, neither will strangers." Mindful of her father's pained expression, she continued, half in fear and half in defiance, to explain the reason for this ruse.

"Honorable parents, I do not wish to be the cause of your unhappiness. More than anything else, I want to attend school in Hangchow. Since girls are not permitted to study along with their brothers, I shall go clothed in a young scholar's gown, my hair combed in masculine style, my slippers fashioned like those worn by boys." The words tumbled out so rapidly, she was breathless.

"I will not bring disgrace upon the family," she promised. "I will not be recognized as a girl, and I shall forever be grateful to you for letting me fulfill my most fervent desire."

"A scheme such as you propose is rash and imprudent," said

her father. "Should the truth ever become known, we would be ridiculed by all our neighbors. Your mother and I will need to discuss the matter carefully. I shall not be able to reach a decision for several days. Until then you must promise to take your meals as before in order to regain your strength. Furthermore, it is your filial duty to abide by whatever decision I may make."

Yingtai gave her promise. If this last desperate attempt to change her father's mind failed, she had no other choices. She dared not permit her hopes to rise, since she knew that for her parents to act contrary to custom and tradition was unthinkable.

Mercifully, Yingtai was not kept in suspense very long. The next morning her father solemnly announced that he would permit her to attend school in Hangchow, but only under certain conditions. She was to be accompanied by her maid who would be disguised as a manservant. Under no condition was she to reveal her own true identity to strangers. She was to devote herself to her studies without distraction. On the day of her sixteenth birthday, she was to return home, at which time her marriage would be arranged to a proper suitor. Yingtai was overjoyed. At once she began to make preparations for her leave-taking. Marriage was something in the distant future. Eager to savor the joy of the present, she gave it little thought.

On the day of her departure, Yingtai awoke at the sound of the first cock crow. From her bed she watched the daylight spread across the sky. Soon she would be on her way to Hangchow. Somewhere on one of the narrow streets of that ancient city was the school where she would be spending the next three years of her life. Lost in a happy reverie, she was startled when a young man entered her room.

"Mistress," he said softly, "it is time for you to get dressed and for us to be on our way if we expect to reach Hangchow before nightfall." Yingtai recognized the voice of her maid, and both girls burst into laughter.

"From now on you must address me as Young Master," Yingtai instructed. "I, in turn, shall refer to you as my manservant."

Yingtai bade farewell to her beloved parents. Her father hid his feelings behind a blank face. Her mother wept.

No one took notice of the two young boys walking through the village streets. It was not unusual to see a scholar accompanied by his servant following close behind, carrying bundles and pieces of luggage. Once beyond the village, there were still miles to cover along winding dusty roads. By midday, though they never stopped to rest, they had progressed only half-way to their destination. The sun was directly overhead, and when they reached the crest of a steep hill, both Yingtai and her maid were tired from the heat and the strain of walking.

"We will stop here and rest for a while," Yingtai said. Looking about for a suitable place to sit in the shade, she noticed a small pavilion. Not until they had come closer did Yingtai become aware of two figures sitting on the benches inside. At first she hesitated to join the strangers. On the other hand, she thought to herself, this may be a good opportunity to test whether she and her maid could pass as boys.

When they entered the pavilion, a young man stood up, bowed and introduced himself. "I am Liang Shanbo," he said, and pointing to his companion, added, "and this is my servant."

Yingtai returned his greeting and replied, "It is a great honor to make your acquaintance. My manservant and I are on our way to Hangchow where I shall be attending school. Would you by any chance be going in the same direction?"

"Indeed, I am, and I in turn would be honored if you would permit me to accompany you." To their delight, they discovered they were both bound for the same school.

The remainder of the journey seemed shorter and more enjoyable. They talked all the way into the city, exchanging information about their homes and their families. Shanbo related that he was fourteen years old and an only child.

"My family," Yingtai told him, "is quite large. I am the

Whenever possible, Shanbo and Yingtai studied together.

youngest of nine brothers and I have just passed my thirteenth birthday. I am the last one to be sent off to study.''

By the time the two new acquaintances arrived, they were drawn together in warm friendship. So comfortable were they in each other's company, they agreed to request lodgings in the same dormitory. Whenever possible, they studied together and spent the little free time they had taking refreshing walks into the countryside. In the three years that followed, the bond between them grew ever stronger and they were never happier than when they were in each other's company.

As the day of her sixteenth birthday drew nearer, Yingtai's normal cheerfulness was replaced by a brooding melancholy. Unnaturally quiet, she kept her troubled thoughts to herself, nor did she confide in her faithful maid. She had fallen in love with her closest friend, but she could not reveal to him that he had captured her heart. The secret that Yingtai carried within her finally became so troublesome, she had to share it with someone.

Mrs. Wang, the wife of the headmaster, was a kind, motherly woman who had on several occasions admired Yingtai for her pleasant manners and exceptional scholarship. It was to Mrs. Wang that Yingtai confessed she was a girl.

"To tell the truth, Yingtai," said the wise older woman, "I have suspected this all along, but since you were such a good student, I kept my silence. To have discussed my suspicions with the headmaster would have led to your immediate dismissal. What a pity to deny so worthy a student the chance for an education!"

"I have yet another problem," confided Yingtai. "I am in love with my friend, Liang Shanbo, but I cannot express my feelings for him. He believes that I am a boy, and to reveal my identity would mean breaking a solemn promise I made to my father." Yingtai could not go on. Her eyes brimmed over.

"What can I do to help you?" Mrs. Wang asked.

"I promised I would return home on the day of my sixteenth

birthday. This was one of the conditions laid down by my father before he would permit me to attend school. Tomorrow I turn sixteen, and I must leave. I cannot face Shanbo, and I would be grateful to you if you would tell him the reason for my abrupt departure. Tell him also that I pray his affection for me will match the tenderness I feel for him. In my happiest dreams I picture myself as his bride.''

Yingtai sighed. With her secret no longer pent up inside her, she felt relieved. Lifting a gold pendant from around her neck, she handed it to Mrs. Wang. "Will you please give this to Shanbo as a token of my sincere friendship?'' Mrs. Wang agreed and wished Yingtai a safe journey home. She assured her that she would deliver all her messages.

On her way out of the dormitory the next morning, Shanbo encountered Yingtai, dressed for travel.

"Aren't you coming to class?'' he asked, surprised. Without offering an explanation, she curtly announced that she had been called home and was to begin her return trip that very day.

"Has there been a death in the family? Has either of your parents been taken ill?'' Short of a family tragedy, Shanbo could not imagine what had brought on this sudden need to leave school. In reply to each of his questions, Yingtai merely shook her head, but said not a word.

"At least,'' he insisted, "let me walk with you as far as the pavilion where good fortune caused us to meet three years ago.''

They walked slowly, each hoping to delay the moment of separation. It was not at all like the first day of their meeting when they had hurried toward Hangchow, looking forward to a new adventure. Somberly, they parted at the pavilion, expressing the hope that they would meet again some day.

After such a long absence, Yingtai's parents were delighted to see their daughter. When she left home she was still a child. Now they welcomed a young woman who had flowered into a beauty. Her father could hardly wait to tell her of his plans.

"My daughter, you are now sixteen and ready for marriage. I have made all the arrangements and have chosen for your future husband the heir of an influential, wealthy family. Your mother and I are pleased with him, and I know he will find favor with you as well. The Ma family, in turn, is happy to welcome you as a daughter-in-law. They think you will make a suitable wife for their son. All that remains is to set the date for the wedding."

Yingtai was too stung by her father's revelation to answer.

"Good, then you agree," said her father. "It is all settled."

Yingtai started to reply, but gave up in despair. To rebel would be shameful, and she had given her word that she would never oppose her father's wishes.

When Shanbo returned to his dormitory he found a note requesting him to report to the headmaster's house. But he had fallen behind in his lessons and had to prepare for an important examination that was to take place the following day. He placed the note to one side on his desk. Two days later, while shuffling through some papers in search of a specific Confucian text, he came upon the note from the headmaster's wife. He went at once to call on her.

"I have a message and a gift for you from your former schoolmate," Mrs. Wang began. "Yingtai asked me to give you this gold pendant on her behalf, and to reveal a secret she has guarded these past three years. Yingtai could not bear to tell you herself that she is a girl, nor could she confess her love for you."

Shanbo felt a surge of happiness flow through him. But his shyness kept him from saying little more than "Thank you," when accepting the gift.

Before he reached his room he had made several decisions. First he would visit his parents and seek their permission to marry Yingtai. Then he would try to see Yingtai and her family.

Several weeks elapsed before Shanbo finally reached Yingtai's village. On the day of his arrival, his fond hopes for a happy reunion were shattered.

"I am sorry," Yingtai's father told him coldly, "but you are too late. Yingtai is already betrothed, and will soon marry a son of the Ma family. Both families have signed a binding contract that cannot be broken."

Shanbo knew then that Yingtai was forever beyond his grasp. He blamed only himself for his misery. Surely he should have seen through Yingtai's disguise. If only he had not been so blind, so trusting. Guilt and remorse gnawed at him until he lost his will to live. His strength ebbed until he grew feeble and frail. Still pining for his love, Shanbo's soul departed the earth.

When the news of Shanbo's death reached Yingtai, she was overcome with grief. Sick at heart, unable to hide her sadness, she remained aloof while the house buzzed with excited preparations for her wedding. Her mother hovered near her, now scolding, now cajoling, trying to keep family peace. She feared that her willful daughter might create an embarrassing scene before the invited guests. But Yingtai made her protest even before they set forth from the house.

"I ask that you grant me just one wish before my marriage," she pleaded with her father. "On the way to my bridegroom's home, I would like my sedan chair to be carried past the tomb of my former school companion. I shall take but a moment to bid him a last farewell."

"Why spoil a joyous wedding procession with such a dreary visit?" her father protested. "You are soon to be a married woman; it is time to forget your girlish infatuation."

Yingtai insisted. "If you deny me this small favor, I shall refuse to marry the man you have chosen to be my husband."

To avoid further unpleasantness Yingtai's father grudgingly gave his consent. Leading the other family members, he stormed out of the house and signaled the procession to begin.

In her red-curtained chair Yingtai was carried toward the Ma family home. There her husband-to-be and his parents awaited

Yingtai's chair was lowered before Shanbo's grave.

her arrival. About her head she had tied a white cloth band, the symbol of mourning for the dead. Her loyal maidservant walked alongside, her head similarly bound. Making their way through the village, they passed beyond the last cluster of houses and reached the cemetery. The attendants swore later that the moment Yingtai's chair was lowered before Shanbo's grave, the freshly heaped burial mound parted. Yingtai hurled herself into the gaping hole. The earth closed above her.

All this happened in the fourth century during the time of the Eastern Jin Dynasty. To this day mourners who worship at the graves of their ancestors can see two butterflies fluttering above Shanbo's tomb. One is a vivid blue with gold markings, the other a pale yellow streaked with black. It is said they are the spirits of the two young lovers, united at last.

The
Palace
Plot

How was it that Jen Dzung, the powerful emperor of the Middle Kingdom who ruled over China with a mandate from heaven, awakened every morning feeling downcast and melancholy? The birds sang in the garden outside his bedroom door, fresh dew glistened in the early rays of the sun, and flowers opened their petals, joyously welcoming the day. But the emperor paid little heed to the beauty around him. He was not content, for he had no heir to inherit his throne.

During the early years of his reign, Emperor Jen Dzung had devoted himself entirely to his far-flung empire and had won high praise for the way he dealt with affairs of state. From the beginning, he had the wisdom to surround himself with loyal ministers and men of great learning. Guided by their wise counsel, he undertook many ambitious projects that brought prosperity and peace to his subjects. He was so preoccupied with official business that he neglected to select a wife. Instead, as was customary, he had taken two concubines, Lady Li and Lady Liu.

Jen Dzung was captivated by Lady Li's dark, almond eyes, by her peach-blossom complexion and rose-bud lips. He admired her shining black hair, piled into an elaborate bun atop her head and held in place by a carved jade comb. Always considerate and gentle, Lady Li was able to soothe the emperor's troubled mind whenever he was in her company.

Lady Liu delighted the emperor with her lively conversation

and high spirits. Her sparkling eyes and bubbling laughter endeared her to him. When he was with her she entertained him by singing sweet songs, accompanying herself on the lute.

The day came when the emperor, older and concerned about the future welfare of his kingdom, summoned them both into his chambers. When they were seated comfortably and had been served a cup of tea, he explained that he wished to speak to them about a matter of great importance.

"My constant worry," he began, "is that I shall have no heir to take my place when I am gone. I think about it night and day, and it grieves me that I do not have a son to follow after me. I have always cherished the hope that my dynasty would continue unbroken for generations. Today," continued Jen Dzung, "an idea has come to me. I believe that my hope can be realized, but only with your cooperation."

Lady Li and Lady Liu glanced at each other. It was plain from the expression on their faces that his talk puzzled them.

Lady Li bowed respectfully. "I am honored, Your Excellency, that you ask for my assistance." Smiling shyly, she added, "I shall be glad to help in any way I can."

"And I, too," agreed Lady Liu, "am always ready to do whatever you ask."

Thus assured, Jen Dzung disclosed his plan to them. "The time has come when I should take a wife. I feel a deep affection for both of you, and I find it impossible to make a choice. Therefore, I have decided that whoever will be first to present me with a male child shall be given the title of Queen, and shall reign beside me on the royal throne."

Emperor Jen Dzung could not foresee that his words would stir up a bitter rivalry between his two concubines, one that would cause untold suffering and claim many victims, he himself among them.

Before long, Lady Li learned that she was pregnant. It was predicted by the court fortune-teller that the child would be a boy.

The emperor was overjoyed, and in appreciation he presented Lady Li with a brooch of gold and precious jewels in the shape of a phoenix.

With the passing of each month, the air of expectation in the palace mounted. In anticipation of the eventful day, elaborate preparations were underway to receive the royal prince.

Lady Liu remained apart. Resentful of the attention centered on Lady Li, she spent most of her time sulking in her own quarters. Bitterness assailed her when she realized she would never sit upon the royal throne. If only there were a way to alter the course of events! She sought out Guo Huai, her favorite palace eunuch. Perhaps he could advise her.

Guo Huai had lived in the palace since he was a child. Sharp of mind, cunning and crafty, he went about ingratiating himself with the emperor by wearing a false smile and catering to Jen Dzung's every whim. Well aware that the emperor favored both Lady Li and Lady Liu, Guo Huai had encouraged their friendship. With Lady Li, who was modest and reserved, he did not succeed, but with the more outgoing Lady Liu, he developed a sympathetic relationship. They conversed frequently, and often found themselves exchanging confidences. So it was perfectly natural for Lady Liu to turn to Guo Huai to unburden herself.

When she poured out her heart, Guo Huai consoled her. "Your sadness pains me, but do not fret any longer. I promise I will think of something to restore your good humor. Even now, as you speak to me, thoughts are forming in my head. Meanwhile, keep a cheerful appearance and let no one suspect that you are troubled."

Guo Huai's confidence encouraged Lady Liu. She trusted him. Still, she worried that something might go awry, exposing both of them to the wrath of the emperor. For her the next few months were filled with anxiety.

The palace gong announced the good news. An heir to the throne had been born. The infant was quickly wrapped in layers of soft cloth and taken to the nursery. Lady Li, worn out by the long, painful labor and feeling very weak, fell asleep immediately. Toward evening when she awoke somewhat refreshed, she asked the nursemaid in attendance to bring her the baby. The nursemaid placed a tightly wrapped bundle on the bed beside Lady Li, who expectantly undid the silken brocade wrapper.

Lady Li stared in disbelief. Instead of a healthy baby boy there lay a jelly-like mass of pink flesh. Green eyes stared unseeing from a shriveled head. Small pointed ears like those of a cat stuck out above the skull. Piercing screams rose from Lady Li's throat and echoed through the rooms of the palace. Her pitiful cries gave way to hysteria, and she lapsed into unconsciousness.

The emperor was informed that Lady Li had given birth to a monster! His disappointment soon turned to anger, and he blamed the poor mother for having produced such an unnatural creature. Declaring that he never wanted to see her again, he banished her to the servants' quarters.

During all this turmoil, Lady Liu and Guo Huai closeted themselves in Lady Liu's sitting room. Several pillows had been arranged on a small bench, and on this makeshift crib an infant was fast asleep. Guo Huai was explaining, ''...and then I killed the cat with one blow, skinned it, patted it dry and wrapped it up. Undetected by anyone, I stole into the nursery and exchanged one bundle for the other.'' Guo Huai smiled with self-satisfaction.

Lady Liu was shaken by the audacity of Guo Huai's scheme. She was now involved in a plot from which she could not extricate herself.

''What am I to do with the baby?'' she cried.

''This is no time for whimpering!'' The brash eunuch was plainly annoyed. His icy tone frightened Lady Liu.

''Have him killed and be done with it,'' he said without a trace of feeling.

Lady Liu felt trapped. Even if she wanted to undo everything that had happened, it was impossible. Finally, when she could think of no alternative, she called for her personal maid, Pearl, and ordered her to drown the baby in the river that ran close to the palace grounds.

Always dutiful, Pearl had never before disobeyed Lady Liu's bidding. Now, as she carried the baby toward the river, rebellion rose within her for the first time. She could not take a life. She could not make herself obey her mistress's instructions. Clutching the infant to her chest, she walked slowly. Her eyes were swollen, her cheeks tear-stained. She felt more wretched with every step. At her wit's end, she sat down on the damp ground. So absorbed was she in her misery she did not hear the sound of approaching footsteps.

Chen Lin, one of the emperor's most trusted eunuchs, was at her side. He was on his way to deliver a bowl of fresh fruit to the emperor's cousin, Duke Jau. "Why are you crying?" Chen Lin asked.

Pearl felt that she need not fear betrayal at Chen Lin's hands. He was respected by everyone in the palace for his high moral character. Haltingly, she told him about the events that had led up to her present plight. The kindly eunuch was shocked by Pearl's story. He found it hard to believe that such vile acts were taking place under the emperor's roof. He helped Pearl to her feet.

"Enough weeping," he said firmly. "It won't do to have someone see you with such red eyes. We must act without delay." A faint cry came from the bundle. The infant was beginning to stir.

Chen Lin loosened the paper seal that secured the cover of the bowl. He quickly removed the cover and discarded the fruit. "Give me the baby," he directed.

"What are you going to do with him?" Pearl asked anxiously.

"I shall take him with me to Duke Jau's house. He and his wife are childless, and I am certain a baby boy will bring joy into their lives. Now, Pearl, you must run back to the palace and tell Lady Liu that you have carried out her orders. Go as fast as you can, and remember, only you and I know the truth."

"Give me the baby," Chen Lin directed.

Chen Lin placed the baby in the bowl and reset the cover lightly. He wiped the sweat from his forehead and hurried on, hoping to reach the Duke's house without incident.

He had not gone very far when directly into his path stepped the huge Guo Huai.

"Have you seen Pearl?" he asked Chen Lin gruffly.

"No, I have not seen her today," Chen Lin replied with dignity.

"What are you carrying in that bowl?" Guo Huai persisted.

"On behalf of the emperor, I am delivering this bowl of fresh fruit to Duke Jau. Today is the duke's birthday." Chen Lin forced himself to smile.

"Give me that bowl," came the haughty demand. "I want to see what is in it myself." Guo Huai tried to grab the bowl out of Chen Lin's firm grasp.

"Have you taken leave of your senses? This bowl was sealed by the emperor and no one but the duke may open it. If you dare touch this bowl once more, I shall report your inexcusable behavior to His Majesty." Chen Lin remained outwardly unperturbed while hiding his inner turmoil.

"Oh, little prince," implored Chen Lin silently, "please do not make a sound, or we shall all be dead." Unsettled by the close call, he walked quickly away without a backward glance.

Duke Jau and his wife welcomed Chen Lin warmly. After an exchange of greetings they asked what had brought him to their house.

Chen Lin held out the bowl and said, "I bring you a gift for your birthday." Duke Jau removed the cover of the bowl. His eyes widened when he saw the tiny infant curled up inside. Before the duke could ask for an explanation, Chen Lin recounted the tragic events that had occurred in the palace.

"I have brought the child here with the hope that in your home he will be sheltered and kept from harm."

The duke and his wife were enchanted with the pink-cheeked

infant. By the time he reached his first year, the child was toddling easily on sturdy legs. At three he could be seen running through the garden chasing crickets and butterflies. From his mother, Lady Li, he had inherited an even temper, and like her, his sweet expression and friendly smile won him the affection of all. His mind flowered early, and when he was six, a fine tutor was hired to begin his training in the classics.

That same year the palace gong rang out a second time to announce good tidings. Lady Liu had given birth to a male child. The emperor rejoiced. He sent off messengers to carry the news to the most distant villages in the land. With all the pomp and splendor befitting such an occasion, Lady Liu was crowned queen.

Unfortunately, the baby sickened and died before he was three months old. A pall settled over the palace. Dispirited by the tragedy, the emperor shut himself in his study and refused to see anyone.

"Now I may never have an heir," he lamented.

Weeks passed and still the emperor continued to mourn. In search of solace, he decided to pay a call on his cousin, Duke Jau. In their youth both men had spent much time together, but due to the press of official business, years had slipped by without their seeing one another.

When the emperor arrived at Duke Jau's home he was cordially received. "It is indeed a great honor that you have come to pay us a visit," said the duke, "and I am grateful that you accept our hospitality."

The duke invited the emperor into the courtyard. The plum trees were at their showiest, each one a large bouquet of white blossoms. The sweet scent of pink peonies perfumed the air. In the midst of this serene landscape the emperor felt less dejected. He and the duke sat in the open pavilion, talking quietly of old times and sipping cups of hot tea.

Their conversation was interrupted by the appearance of a

young boy who, the emperor assumed, was the duke's son. Accompanied by his tutor, the boy was about to take his daily walk in the fresh air. The emperor was completely taken by the handsome child.

Turning to Duke Jau, the emperor said ruefully, "For years I have cherished the hope of having an heir, and that wish is yet unfulfilled. I would gladly part with half my kingdom if only I could be blessed with a son like yours." The emperor hesitated. He chose his words carefully. "Would you be willing to allow the boy to come and live with me in the palace as my adopted son? I shall issue an official proclamation declaring that he will inherit the throne when I die. For the remaining years of my life I shall be content knowing that the dynasty will continue unbroken."

The emperor's request placed Duke Jau in an awkward predicament. He would have liked to reveal the truth about the boy. To disclose the palace plot, however, would implicate Queen Liu, and he doubted that his word would hold against her denial. To complicate matters further, he and his wife had grown extremely fond of the emperor's son. "We will miss him," Duke Jao thought sadly. But a royal request was a royal command. He had no choice.

"Your Majesty," he offered, nodding respectfully, "my wife and I are honored to grant your wish."

The boy was given over to the care of Queen Liu. At first she shared the emperor's joy. He had found a successor to the throne, and she had been given another chance to raise a son. But her happiness was short-lived, for almost immediately she noticed the strong resemblance the child bore to Lady Li. Buried memories came back to trouble her. She could not sleep, for her dreams were nightmares.

Once more Queen Liu sent for her loyal friend, Guo Huai, and told him of her growing qualms.

"What do you think I should do?" she questioned him tearfully. "How can we learn the truth?"

Guo Huai found the turn of events alarming. He recalled how Chen Lin had refused to open the bowl when they met along the river path. Could it be that the wily eunuch had deceived him and that Queen Liu's suspicions were justified? Dire thoughts raced through his head.

"Send for Pearl at once," he proposed, "and also for Chen Lin."

Within minutes, Pearl entered the chamber, followed by Chen Lin. Queen Liu wasted no time.

"Did you carry out my orders to drown Lady Li's baby?" she demanded of Pearl.

"Yes, Your Majesty," Pearl lied.

"Did you tell anyone about it?"

"Not a soul," she lied again, but her voice was beginning to tremble.

"Were you careful not to be seen?"

Pearl began to stammer a reply, but when she saw Guo Huai's piercing eyes fixed on her, she fell silent.

"Well," said Guo Huai, "if she will not talk, there is a way to loosen her tongue. A good beating often brings on a confession. May I suggest, Your Majesty, that you direct Chen Lin to apply a few strokes with bamboo rods. The pain in her back will hasten words from her mouth."

Queen Liu was desperate enough to fall in with this brutal idea, and Chen Lin had no choice but to comply. Not wanting to cause Pearl much pain, he picked up the rods and struck her lightly several times across the back. Guo Huai's steely eyes narrowed. "Harder," he shouted.

Chen Lin obeyed most unwillingly, and Pearl's wailing filled the chamber.

"That is not hard enough," raged Guo Huai. In a fit of fury he grabbed the rods out of Chen Lin's hand. Mercilessly, he rained blow after blow upon the hapless Pearl. "Now speak," he threatened. "You will not be spared unless you tell the truth. Did you drown the baby?'' Pearl's lips remained sealed. Guo Huai bore down even harder, whipping the screaming Pearl until she crumpled at his feet.

"Enough, enough," cried Queen Liu. She was appalled by Guo Huai's ruthlessness and demanded he put down the rods. But it was too late. Pearl slowly raised her head. She looked directly at her tormentors and, in a barely audible voice, uttered her last words.

"You evil-minded devils, some day you will be punished for your wicked ways." A groan escaped her lips as she fell back on the floor. She had ceased to breathe.

Chen Lin understood that Queen Liu and Guo Huai would not be satisfied with just one victim. Fearing they would plan next to do away with Lady Li, he rushed to the servants' quarters to look for her. He found her at work in the kitchen, took her aside, and related all that had happened after the birth of her child.

"You must flee the palace," he warned, "for your life is in danger." He escorted her to safety beyond the palace gate and wished her good luck.

Outside the palace walls, Lady Li, once the beloved confidant of the emperor, was reduced to begging. With nothing but the clothes on her back, deprived of the flimsiest shelter, she determined to survive against all odds. "The time will come," she comforted herself, "when justice will prevail."

Emperor Jen Dzung reigned for ten more years before his allotted time on earth came to an end. He never learned that the boy whom he had adopted was his own son. With traditional pageantry, he was buried in an ornate tomb. In an equally splendid ceremony, the young emperor was seated on the throne and became the new ruler of China.

At that time there lived a shrewd but righteous judge known for his ability to solve the most difficult of cases. One day, when he was being carried across a small bridge leading to the palace gates, a disheveled dirty woman ran out in front of his sedan chair.

"Injustice, injustice!" she screamed. "The Queen Mother is an impostor. I am the emperor's mother, and I have evidence to prove it."

The judge's curiosity was aroused and he motioned for his sedan chair to be set down. He spoke to his guard.

"Let the ragged beggar come closer so I can hear what it is that she wants."

"Your Excellency, I beg your indulgence," the woman pleaded. Her tone was now much quieter and she spoke with proper humility. "A great injustice was done to me many years ago. I am the true mother of the young emperor. Here, Your Excellency, is my proof." She handed the judge a small gold brooch in the shape of a phoenix. A gift such as this could only be bestowed by the emperor. "How could it have come into the hands of this dirty beggar?" the judge wondered.

"Bring the woman to my office," directed the judge, and he gave the signal to move on.

That afternoon he was busy at his writing table when Lady Li was brought in. Politely, the judge asked her to be seated.

"You may leave us alone," he said, dismissing the guard.

The judge listened with fascination to Lady Li's woeful tale. She told him how she had been mistreated and how she had been deprived of her child. Several times in the course of her narration she had to stop to fight back her tears.

The judge considered this a matter of extreme gravity. Since members of the royal family were involved, he would have to handle the situation with the utmost delicacy. All the facts had to be established before informing the emperor.

The inquiry was begun by questioning Guo Huai. Naturally, the sly eunuch denied everything.

"You are willing to believe this deranged tramp instead of me," he protested. "You will never be able to prove so outrageous a charge."

"Very well," the judge replied. "The woman may be deranged as you say, but until she is proven wrong I must hold you under arrest."

The judge's reputation for wisdom was well deserved, for he soon thought of an extraordinary plan. He had his courtroom rearranged to resemble a courtroom in hell. Incense was burned for hours, and a dense smoke hung heavily in the air. The court attendants were dressed in animal skins, grotesque masks of horned cow heads and full-maned horse heads hiding their faces.

When all the preparations were complete, the judge asked the warden to send a bottle of good wine and a bowl of delicious food to Guo Huai's cell.

"Tell the eunuch that the queen sends him a gift," the judge instructed a guard. Guo Huai was heartened by this lenient treatment. He took it as a sign that the queen would use her influence on his behalf and have him freed. With his stomach full of food and wine, he fell asleep, snoring loud enough to be heard throughout the jail.

At the stroke of midnight, his slumber was rudely shattered by the beating of bass drums. He sat up with a start. The drumbeats became faster and louder until he felt that his head was about to explode.

Then, above the din rose a blood-curdling shriek. Fully alert and very frightened, Guo Huai heard his name being called. Near him towered two masked attendants, their heads looking even more hideous as their horns cast elongated shadows on the walls. Guo Huai believed he was surely going mad.

The drums stopped suddenly. Out of the darkness came a low menacing voice.

"The day of justice has arrived. You will pay for all your past sins. You are condemned to suffer the tortures of hell and there will be no escape."

The roll of the drums sounded again. Guo Huai was jerked to

Iron chains were wound around Guo Hai's neck.

his feet, and iron chains were wound around his neck. The attendants dragged him out of his cell, down the middle aisle of the long courtroom, and stood him before the judge. Now the eunuch was convinced he had awakened in Satan's domain.

"Bring Pearl into the courtroom," bellowed the judge. Clad in the white robes of death, long black hair covering her face, a woman was led in. With slow deliberate steps she walked toward Guo Huai. The terrified eunuch recoiled as she came closer, and he would have fled had not the guards barred his way. In a high-pitched strident voice she accused him of unspeakable crimes.

"I am Pearl, the innocent maid you mercilessly beat to death. I have come to take my revenge. Your evil deeds have been disclosed, your villainy unmasked. Before the Judge of Hell, I charge you, Guo Huai, of plotting to kill the emperor's son."

"Please, Your Excellency," cried Guo Huai, falling to his knees. "It was not my fault. I was only following Queen Liu's orders." Words gushed from his mouth. When everything he had to say was properly recorded and his signature duly affixed, the judge ordered torches to be lit. The courtroom was flooded with light. Only then did Guo Huai realize that he had been tricked into confession.

For his treachery Guo Huai was sentenced to death. He was executed on the night of the next full moon.

The wise judge continued to serve in the circle of the emperor's most loyal advisors. Those who were tempted to indulge in misdeeds desisted, knowing full well they would be found out and made to pay for their crimes. Thus justice prevailed throughout the land.

Tormented by remorse, Queen Liu fell ill. Secluded in her bedchamber, she would take neither food nor drink. She languished, and before the month ended, death claimed her.

The young emperor bestowed upon Lady Li the title of Queen Mother. Their reunion brought both of them great joy, and the emperor spared nothing to make his mother's life so pleasurable that in time she forgot her past suffering. With prudence and compassion he ruled for many years, earning the respect and devotion of his subjects.

A palace plot has come undone,
A mighty judge the truth has won,
An inglorious end the wicked met,
A dynasty, its course is set.
The rightful king all subjects hail,
Evil deeds will not prevail.

Monkey

On the mountain of flowering fruit, in the distant land of Aolai, a remarkable rock lay hidden among tangled, windblown shrubs. Over the countless centuries, the sun, the moon, and the earth combined forces to develop, deep within the heart of the rock, a magic egg. At exactly the right moment a bolt of lightning split the rock asunder. The egg, released from its marble imprisonment, rolled along the ground and came to rest beneath the sheltering branches of a towering pine tree. From this egg, out into the world, burst an indestructible stone monkey. Safe from harm, the monkey grew stronger, leaped higher, was brighter, braver, and bolder than any other of his tribe. He was also more mischievous.

Unburdened by fear, the stone monkey braved unknown perils to find a safe haven where he and his friends could lead a blissful existence. Lacking modesty, he proclaimed himself the Monkey King and joyfully reigned over his obedient subjects.

With the passage of time his happiness faded, for his dear friends grew old and, one by one, were laid to rest. The Monkey King became fretful and morose. "Someday I, too, shall become weak and ill, and death will claim me," he lamented. His days were filled with dreary thoughts until he learned that the gift of eternal life was bestowed upon sages and buddhas. Quickly he made up his mind. He would study and become a holy man.

Monkey set forth on a search that was to take him thousands of miles from home. After years of wandering, he came upon a scholarly teacher who reluctantly agreed to instruct him in religious doctrine.

"I do not have much hope for your success," the venerable patriarch told him at their first meeting. "You do not know how to dress, your manners are crude, and you are extremely ugly. But if you mend your ways and behave yourself, I shall permit you to join my school of disciples, on probation."

Monkey proved to be an apt student. Within months he learned to choose the correct attire, to eat without spilling a drop, to bow properly before his superiors. Applying himself to his studies, he memorized hundreds upon hundreds of scriptural laws. Still, he was not satisfied with his progress until he had mastered the art of transforming himself into seventy-two different shapes, and had learned how to traverse the sky by hopping from cloud to cloud. But try as he might, Monkey could not suppress his frolicsome spirit forever. When he disrupted the tranquility of the school by entertaining the other disciples with his magic tricks, he infuriated the old master and earned a proper scolding.

"I knew the moment I set eyes on you that no good would come of this. You are not here to enjoy yourself, you are here only to study."

"I like to have fun, sometimes," retorted Monkey sassily. "Besides, it is very boring here. I have already learned everything there is to learn. Once I become a sage, and immortal, I shall depart."

Realizing that there was only one way to rid himself of this thorn in his side, the learned master was quick to bestow upon Monkey the title of sage, send him away, and restore harmony to his school.

Monkey returned home, leaping from one billowy cloud to another. He gathered all the other monkeys around him and declared that henceforth he was to be addressed as Great Immortal Sage.

In his exalted position he was waited on by a host of servants. With little to do, he idled away hour after hour. The Jade Emperor, all-knowing monarch of heaven, was wise to expect that Monkey, with so much time on his hands, would get into trouble. He decided to appoint him guardian of the heavenly peach garden, thus giving him a task of considerable responsibility.

Now if the Jade Emperor had not put Monkey in charge of the peach garden, and if the Queen of Heaven had not neglected to invite him to her peach banquet, all would have gone well. His feelings hurt by what he thought to be a royal snub, Monkey ran amok. He broke the furniture, smashed the dishes, ate the peaches, and drank so much wine he fell into a drunken stupor. For his unseemly behavior, he was severely punished. Wedged between two huge flat rocks near the top of a windy, desolate mountain, he was left to mull over his misdeeds.

The Jade Emperor did not enjoy meting out punishment. Though quick to discipline wrongdoers, he always held out the chance of forgiveness. "If you are truly repentant a day may come," he promised Monkey, "when you will be set free."

Five hundred years were to pass before the promise was fulfilled. It happened that Tang Seng, a devout monk riding astride a white horse, was on his way west to fetch the Buddhist scriptures from far-off India. Crossing over the mountain, he was attracted by weak cries for help. He dismounted and came closer to discover poor Monkey peering out through a slit in his cramped jail. Tang Seng was a compassionate man. Moved by Monkey's suffering, he tried to comfort him.

"I shall pray on your behalf," he said, "but I cannot assure you that my prayers will sway heaven." Lifting his face toward the sky, Tang Seng began to recite the sacred sutras. Monkey strained to hear the quiet prayers. Before long he grew impatient and was about to complain that praying was a waste of time, when the rocks that held him fell away.

Released at last, Monkey was forever grateful. He became Tang Seng's constant companion, his guide and protector on the long and arduous route to the west.

Early one evening, tired and weary after traveling for seven days without seeing a single soul, Monkey and Tang Seng came upon a small village. "Let us stop here and rest for the night," suggested Tang Seng.

"I'll go on ahead and make sure it is a proper place for us to stay," offered Monkey, anxious that no mishap befall his master.

Monkey returned, pleased. "It is a pretty village with many well-built cottages, beautiful flowers everywhere, and bamboo growing thickly along a clear stream. At the edge of the village there is a well-kept farm. If the farmer is a considerate, hospitable man, he will not turn us away."

They did not yet know that the farm belonged to a Mr. Gau, who was at that very moment berating his servant, Tsai, for failing to carry out his orders. He had sent Tsai in search of an exorcist to rid his farm of a demon. On three previous occasions Tsai had brought back monks from the local monastery, but each had failed in his efforts to produce the desired results.

"I'll give you one more chance," Gau threatened. "If you do not return with the right exorcist this time, you will be dismissed with a smart beating as a farewell gift."

Tsai packed his belongings in a bundle, picked up his umbrella, and walked out the front gate. He noticed two figures coming toward him. In the lead was a small but agile monkey clad in bright pink pantaloons topped by a yellow sash. His blue jacket was richly trimmed with red braid. From behind his ear gleamed a shiny object that looked like a long needle. Following him was a dignified monk of noble bearing seated stiffly upon a white horse. Two blue ribbons attached to the crown of his hat hung down over his cloak.

Tsai tried to slip by them unnoticed. Such peculiar people would be of no use to him. But suddenly a furry arm grabbed him about the neck so tightly he could not breathe.

"Hold on there! You seem to be in a dreadful hurry. Who are you, and where are you going?"

"Who I am and wither I am bound is of no interest to you. Now let me pass." Struggling in vain to free himself, Tsai dropped his umbrella, and his bundle fell to the ground.

"What is the name of this place?" Monkey screamed directly into Tsai's ear, while Tsai, fighting desperately for each breath, tried to extricate himself from Monkey's chokehold.

"Monkey," called Tang Seng from his perch atop his patient steed, "here comes another person. We can ask him. Let this one go."

Monkey smiled. "You do not understand, Master. It will not be as interesting to ask someone else." Monkey loosened his grip and let Tsai inhale a bit of air.

"Damn it," Tsai spluttered, "I not only have to suffer my master's temper, but I have to put up with the likes of you." He straightened himself and glared angrily at Monkey.

Monkey was suspicious. "You are not dressed for a short trip. I bet you are running away. You had better speak with a civil tongue or I'll make a heap of trouble for you." With a menacing grimace, Monkey displayed his long, sharp teeth, frightening Tsai into replying.

"This is the farm of the Gau family, and I am Tsai, Gau's servant. He has sent me on an important errand, and I must let no one interfere."

"What kind of errand?" persisted Monkey, softening his tone. He hoped that a more reasonable approach would encourage the confused Tsai to speak freely. "Do not be afraid of us. We are pilgrims from the east, journeying to the west in search of the holy Buddhist scriptures. We come in peace and seek to harm no one."

Tsai felt relieved, and explained. "My master has given me money to find an exorcist with magic powers who will be able to remove a demon living in our house. He has shamed my master and upset the neighbors. Worse still, he has locked away the

Tsai glared angrily at Monkey.

master's youngest daughter, and she has not been seen or heard from in months. Three times I returned with those who claimed they would succeed, and three times they failed. For their efforts one received a blackened eye, the second a broken wrist, and the third a kick to the seat of his pants. If I do not return with a more skillful exorcist this time, I will be banished.''

Monkey chortled. ''Well, then, today is your lucky day. That's just my kind of job. I love to chase demons.'' Monkey rubbed his hands together gleefully. ''Leave it to me and the deed is as good as done. What's more, you will not have to pay for my services.''

Tsai was not convinced. ''You are just a small monkey. How could you capture a monster? The one that plagues us is so strong no one can match his strength.''

''We are not just ordinary mortals,'' Monkey assured him.

''I still do not believe you,'' Tsai sneered. He tried to push Monkey aside and continue on his way.

Monkey did not budge. Pulling a hair out of his thigh, he said, ''Change!'' Monkey vanished. In his place stood the tallest and thickest pine tree Tsai had ever seen. A moment passed. The pine tree was gone, and Monkey reappeared, an impish grin stretched from ear to ear.

That was enough for Tsai. He started to walk back toward the house and motioned Tang Seng and Monkey to follow him. When they came to the front gate, Tsai asked them politely to wait until he could inform his master of their arrival.

Tsai had barely stepped into the room when Gau started hurling curses at him. ''You half-wit, imbecile, why haven't you gone to look for an exorcist? What are you doing back here so soon?''

''Master, by good chance I have encountered two travelers journeying to India. One of them possesses uncommon powers and vows he can rid your home of the demon. Furthermore, he asks no payment for his services.''

''Well, if they are travelers from afar they must be wise, and if they do not ask for money, that is still better. Show them in.''

While Tsai went to fetch the strangers, Gau hurried to his bedroom to change his clothes. He put on his best silk robe and, properly adorned, he was ready to receive his visitors.

Tsai ushered in the stately Tang Seng. Before proper introductions could be completed, in dashed Monkey.

"Where is the demon?" he inquired of the startled Gau. The old man shrank back, repulsed by Monkey's frightful features.

"What have you brought me?" he exploded at Tsai. "Isn't it enough to have one demon in this house?"

"But Master, you surprise me," offered Monkey, smiling and shaking his head. "A man of your years should have acquired wisdom with age and know enough not to judge a person by his looks."

Playfully, Monkey removed the shiny needle from behind his ear, made a magic sign, and the needle turned into a golden cudgel. Monkey swung the heavy club once above his head before it evaporated. The needle rested again behind Monkey's ear.

"Who are you?" gasped Gau.

This time Tang Seng took it upon himself to answer. "We are on a holy mission to India. Though we have traveled for many days, a long journey still lies ahead before we reach our destination. It is almost nightfall and we are footsore and weary. With your kind permission, we would like to rest here overnight."

"So that is your game, just to find free lodgings! And what about my demon?" Gau asked crossly.

Monkey laughed. "Ah, you've got it all wrong. We do wish to stay here, but I am just itching to go after your demon. May I ask how many of these monsters reside in your house? The more the merrier."

"Heaven protect us," said Gau. "How many monsters do I need? There is only one and he is driving me mad."

"Please, sir, try to remain calm. If you will tell us the whole story without leaving out a single detail, I will guarantee to take care of your monster to your complete satisfaction."

No longer so wary, Gau addressed his guests graciously. "Be seated, gentlemen. Please accept my hospitality. As you already know, my name is Gau, and my farm is one of the most prosperous in the area. My fields of rich, dark loam are well watered. Each spring I sow my seeds, assured that at the end of summer a field of golden wheat will ripen and ripple in the breeze. For many years I arose each morning eager to pick up my tools and begin my chores. But age took its toll, and my boundless energy waned. My back ached, my arms felt heavy, my legs weak. I needed someone young and strong to assist me."

"What a windbag," thought Monkey. "Get to the point, Master Gau," he urged. "What of the demon?"

"Yes, of course. My wife and I have three lovely daughters, but to our sorrow, no sons. The two eldest girls, Fragrant Orchid and Jade Orchid, have married into neighboring families, and we enjoy frequent visits with our newly acquired relatives. By the time our youngest daughter, Green Orchid, was ready for marriage, I knew I had to find a son-in-law willing to work on the farm.

"As luck would have it, a young man showed up one day. He related that his home was near Fuling Mountain, that he had no living kinfolk and that he was anxious to find a place to work. Hard labor, he assured me, was what he liked best, and he would be willing to marry my daughter in exchange for being taken into the family. He seemed a rather honest sort and was of a pleasant appearance. I was satisfied. An arrangement such as this was just what I had in mind."

"But what of the demon?" Monkey asked again. Patience was not one of his virtues.

Gau continued his narrative. "For three years the young man did not disappoint me. Pushing the plow unaided, reaping the wheat with his bare hands, he increased my riches tenfold. Then a puzzling change began to overtake him. His nose broadened until it resembled a snout with pink, flaring nostrils. His cheeks became pendulous jowls, his eyes, tiny beads peeking through folds of flesh. Along the back of his neck sprouted stiff, ugly bristles. His resemblance to a hog was so marked he soon earned the nickname, Pigsy.

"Pigsy's appetite was enormous, consuming at each meal five pounds of rice and one hundred steamed buns. For no reason at all, he would cause wild winds to whip through the air, disturbing the peaceful lives of the villagers. Then without giving reason or explanation, he locked Green Orchid in a shed at the rear of the property. My wife and I have not seen her for six months. We fear she may have become ill; worse yet, that she may be close to death."

"It seems to me that your demon may not be such a bad chap after all," suggested Monkey. "A man who works hard deserves to be well fed, and since you married him to your daughter, he has a perfect right to do with her as he pleases."

This was not what Gau wished to hear. Desperate, he begged, "You must help me. This Pigsy is a fiend, a brute, a devil. We tremble for our daughter's safety. I implore you to save her."

"You are too critical," chided Monkey. "After all, a hard-working son-in-law is more valuable than a useless daughter."

"But that monster is destroying my reputation," Gau whined, "and he is without relatives. There is no one to visit and no one to talk to."

"Now that's a reasonable complaint," remarked Monkey. "A reputation is a hard thing to lose, and having no relatives to visit is indeed a worse calamity."

"Thank you. Then we are of one mind." Monkey's sarcasm escaped Gau's understanding. "When do you plan to track down the rascal?"

"I could start now," said Monkey, "but it would be best to wait until after dark. First you must send your servant to care for my master's horse, and then you must provide my master with pleasant company for the evening."

"It shall be done, but what kind of weapon would you like?" Gau asked, trying to be helpful. "I can provide a sharp-bladed axe or a heavy stick."

"Never mind, I have my own weapons, no need for more," Monkey assured him.

After dinner, Monkey followed Gau to a shed behind the house. The moon lit their way as they walked toward a dark corner of the yard.

"How are you going to get in?" Gau questioned anxiously. "The door has a copper lock and I have no key."

"Don't worry about that. It's easy." Instantly the shiny needle behind Monkey's ear was again transformed into the golden cudgel. Monkey used it to smash the lock, then kicked the door open.

Straining to see into the darkness, Gau called, "Daughter, I do not see you. Are you there? Are you all right?"

"Father," came the weak reply. "Is it really you?" Green Orchid rose from the bed and staggered toward Gau, sobbing. "I am so glad you have come at last."

"My poor child, how thin you are! What has that evil husband of yours done to you?"

"Oh, father, it has been so wretched, penned up like an animal in a cage. Pigsy gave me so little to eat my cheeks have become hollow, my flesh has melted away."

Gau tried to comfort his daughter. "Dry your tears, little daughter. We shall soon be rid of the villain who has visited so much pain on us all."

Monkey felt pity for Green Orchid. "You are free to go now, but first, tell me where is your husband?"

"He leaves early every morning and does not return until late at night. He knows father is trying to get rid of him so he stays out of sight."

"Take your daughter back to the house and leave the rest to me," advised Monkey. Then he shut the door from the inside, changed himself into a young girl and crept under the quilt. Wide awake, his ear cocked for the faintest sound, he waited for Pigsy's arrival.

It was almost midnight when Monkey heard someone fumbling at the lock. The door squeaked open and closed, but not before a gust of wind blew in, stirring up a cloud of dust. Without turning on a lamp Pigsy undressed and pulled back the covers. He eased himself onto the bed and moved closer to Monkey. Monkey groaned. Pigsy snuggled up even closer, and threw his arm around Monkey. Monkey pushed him away with such force Pigsy was alarmed.

"What is the matter with you tonight, dear girl? Are you angry because I am later than usual?" he wanted to know.

"Oh, no," answered Monkey, affecting Green Orchid's high-pitched voice.

"Then why are you pushing me away?" Pigsy was beginning to lose his temper.

"I'm feeling ill tonight. Otherwise I would have gotten up to greet you."

"That's no excuse," said Pigsy gruffly. Once again he reached out to caress his wife, but this time no one was there. Monkey, back to his natural self, had silently jumped out of bed and landed on top of an empty barrel.

"Where are you?" cried Pigsy, feeling about the bed in vain.

"I am so unhappy, so long-suffering," whined a girlish voice.

"What are you complaining about? You never acted this way before. Do I not plow and plant all day, drain the ditches, build brick walls? In truth, I earn more than I eat and receive little thanks for my labors."

"You are so misshapen I cannot bear to look at you. You don't have proper manners, and you have ruined my family's reputation," wailed Monkey. "My father has vowed to remove you from our home, and he has hired an exorcist who will rid us of your presence."

"He'll never succeed!" Pigsy laughed out loud. "With my nine-pronged rake, not even the master of all the devils who dwell in the ninth layer of heaven can hurt me. And if you do not return to bed," he threatened, "I'll come and get you!" With this, Pigsy threw off the quilt, leaped out of bed and caught Monkey in a tight embrace. As if stung, Pigsy let go and sprang backward.

"Why are you wearing a fur coat? It is not cold in here."

Monkey positioned himself in front of the window where Pigsy could see him clearly in the moonlight. Brandishing his cudgel, he warned, "You are about to be exorcised by the Monkey King, the Great Immortal Sage, who, five hundred years ago, wreaked havoc among the gods."

Frightened, Pigsy created a swirling dust storm, hiding himself in its center. He flew round and round the room, Monkey soaring after him, flailing the air with his golden cudgel.

"I know you are there, and though you hide among all the clouds of heaven and all the fires of hell, you cannot escape."

Suddenly, the wind died down. Pigsy grabbed his nine-pronged rake and stood before Monkey, poised to pierce him through and through. Monkey, arms akimbo, held his ground with a smirk on his face. Pigsy poked him in the belly, jabbed at his eyes, struck him across the shoulders, and banged him over the head. The nine-pronged rake made nary a dent. Then Monkey delivered a single whack to Pigsy's midriff with his club. Pigsy doubled over, groaning with pain. Mustering what little strength he had left, Pigsy straightened himself. He staggered around on wobbly legs until he regained his balance.

"I give up. I give up. You are too strong for me."

Monkey lunged for him again, but Pigsy would have no more of it. Like a whirlwind, he flew out the door. With Monkey at his heels, he made straight for Fuling Mountain, and never stopped until he reached the entrance to his cave house. Wheezing and panting, he turned around to confront Monkey. But this time, only with words.

Monkey flailed the air with his golden cudgel.

"Why are you chasing me as though I were your enemy? What harm have I ever done to you?"

Monkey shrugged his shoulders. "In truth, you have done me no harm, but I just love to catch demons; it's my favorite pastime." Monkey pulled a hair from his leg and blew on it. Instantly, it turned into a length of thick hemp rope. He used it to bind Pigsy's hands behind his back.

Pigsy continued to argue. "If it is my father-in-law who put you up to this mischief, I do not understand why. I have made him a rich man, married and cared for his daughter. A son-in-law such as I is hard to find. Why should he want to get rid of me?"

Ignoring his chatter, Monkey tied another piece of rope around Pigsy's waist. "Let's go," Monkey said, tugging at him. "I'm taking you back to Gau's farm, and he will do with you as he pleases."

"Tell me, Monkey," asked Pigsy after they had walked a while, "what brought you to Gau's farm in the first place? You are not from these parts."

"I am escorting my master, Tang Seng, to India."

"Did you say Tang Seng? What a coincidence! It was foretold that I would some day meet a monk by that very name, and that I would accompany him on his way to the west."

"I don't believe a single word of it."

"I swear before Buddha that I tell the truth. If I am lying, may my head be severed from my body."

"That would not be a great loss," chuckled Monkey.

"On such a perilous journey," persisted Pigsy, "I can be helpful should you meet with misfortune along the way."

"Well, we may need someone with a strong back to carry our provisions. Come along, we will let Tang Seng be the judge."

That Tang Seng granted Pigsy's wish we can believe. Three odd companions were seen wending their way toward the west. One was a monkey with a shiny needle tucked behind his ear, a second sat astride a white horse. The third, with a nine-pronged rake slung over his shoulder, tagged along, bent under the weight of a large chest strapped to his back.

And so in the end, everything turned out for the best. Gau was free of his demon, Pigsy turned an enemy into a friend, Monkey had a new comrade, and the pious monk gained another disciple.

Cowherd
and
Weaving
Maid

In that part of China where the hills roll gently and swift-running brooks wind through green fields, a small village lay nestled in a peaceful valley. Here a lonely young boy, orphaned at an early age, came to live in the home of his older brother and sister-in-law. They grudgingly allowed him to lay his straw sleeping mat in a corner of the kitchen and to store his few belongings in a splintered wooden box. Never fond of exerting herself, his brother's wife took advantage of her unfortunate charge by heaping upon him all the daily chores. He swept the floor, cleaned the stove, chopped and brought in wood for the fire, carried the water from the well, and weeded the vegetable garden. His most important job was tending the cow, and because of this he was called Cowherd.

Cowherd was kept so busy he did not have time for boyish play. His brother rarely spoke to him, and his grumpy sister-in-law always scolded and found fault, no matter what he did. Without friends his own age, he turned to his gentle cow for companionship. He fed her the tenderest of green grass, then led her to a rushing creek to drink of its sparkling clear water. When the days were hot, he found a place for her to rest in a shady glen where the tree branches formed a sheltering roof overhead. Often he would sit near her, stroking her brown, velvety skin. Taking care not to hurt him with her curving horns, the grateful cow would nudge him with her wet muzzle. When he talked to her she would switch her tail and moo softly in response.

Year after year passed uneventfully, and then, on the day of Cowherd's seventeenth birthday, his boyhood came to an abrupt end.

It was early spring and Cowherd was busily chopping firewood. He did not notice that his sister-in-law had come out of the house until he heard her speak to him sharply.

"Cowherd," she began, "your brother and I have cared for you since you were eight years old. Out of the kindness of our hearts we have provided you with food and lodging for these many years. And you," she accused, "have given us nothing in return. Today you are seventeen, a grown man, old enough to make your own way. We can no longer care for you," she railed on. "Another mouth to feed is a hardship for us." She started to walk off, then stopped to give an order. "By tomorrow morning you are to gather your clothes and leave!"

Cowherd was stunned. He had learned from sad experience not to expect love or even simple kindness from his brother and sister-in-law. But after all he had done for them, he never dreamed that he would be turned out of the only home he knew. On the verge of tears, he asked, "How can you send me into the world, alone and penniless? I have worked hard and long, day after day, to please you. Sister-in-law, I do not understand why you are so cruel to me."

His sister-in-law, feeling only the smallest pang of guilt, responded in a softer tone. "You may take your cow with you if you wish. She is of no use to us, a stubborn beast who will not obey simple commands, and, besides, finding fodder for her will be a nuisance." She hurried away, leaving Cowherd shaken and uneasy about the future.

Early the next morning, Cowherd bundled his tattered clothing into a sack and left the house. Frightened, not knowing where to turn, he wandered through the forest with his cow until they came to a rock-strewn stream, where, in the past, they had spent many contented hours. Without delay he began gathering driftwood and branches to build a lean-to that would protect them from the rain and wind. As soon as he finished the rude shelter, he cleared a piece of land for a vegetable garden. With a short stick he scratched a few furrows, then scattered a handful of seeds on the moist earth. Until he could harvest some beans and cabbages, he and his cow would have to survive as best they could.

The cow found grass to eat wherever the forest thinned, and Cowherd existed on berries and wild plants he knew to be safe. The running stream provided them with good water to drink, and occasionally the rare delicacy of a small fish.

In time, by his working without pause, his vegetable patch began to yield enough for their daily meals. Now and then Cowherd would stop to speak to his beloved cow, who rarely left his side. It was not an easy life they led, and they were quite alone, but they were not unhappy.

One evening, just as the red glow of sunset was disappearing beyond the horizon, Cowherd, tired and weary from his daily labors, stretched out on the ground to rest. He lay on his back and watched the first stars flicker in the darkening sky. His eyelids felt heavy, and he was just about to doze off into sweet slumber when he heard a gruff, scratchy voice whisper his name.

"Cowherd, Cowherd," the voice called. At first Cowherd thought he was dreaming, but after a moment the voice came again, this time louder and more persistent.

"Wake up, Cowherd, I must speak to you."

Cowherd sat bolt upright, wide awake. He glanced in every direction but saw only his cow. He stood up and took a few cautious steps in one direction, then in another. Nothing! Then, in earnest, he started to search everywhere, between the trees, behind rocks, around tall bushes, but he found no one. "Perhaps the voice is just a trick of my imagination," he reasoned with himself. "I must be overtired." Once more he lay down and shut his eyes. Within seconds he heard the voice again.

"Pay heed to what I am about to tell you," it insisted. Cowherd gaped in astonishment. Why, it was his own cow talking to him!

"Tomorrow," explained the cow, "a fairy named Weaving Maid and her sisters will be coming to bathe in the upper stream. They will take off their garments before they enter the water. You must snatch up the pink gown that belongs to Weaving Maid. Keep it well hidden. When she finishes her bath she will look for it, for she must have her gown before she can fly back to heaven. You will present yourself before her and promise to return it only if she consents to marry you."

"But why have I been chosen for so strange a task?" There was no reply.

Cowherd arose before sunup after a night of tossing and turning. He washed his hands and face, combed his hair, and tried to smooth the wrinkles from his old tunic. Not until he had made himself presentable did he set out in the direction of the upper stream. He took the precaution of tying the cow to a tree so she would not follow him. Longingly she watched him disappear into the dense woods. A little later, just as he emerged from the forest, the sound of rushing water reached his ears. Cowherd had frequently strolled along the banks of the upper stream. He knew the location of each boulder that lay exposed above the flowing water. He marvelled to see wiggling tadpoles by the hundreds swim about in shallow pools along the bank. Here he had found comfort and serenity when his spirits were low.

Today, however, he was not calm. The more he thought of the cow's message, the more jittery he became.

A few more steps and he heard a burst of merry laughter. Weaving Maid and her sisters were splashing about with delight under a cascading waterfall.

Crouching behind a tree, Cowherd saw their garments scattered in disarray. The fairies had disrobed in a hurry, carelessly dropping their gowns wherever they stood. A green one was left on the ground, a yellow one lay in a heap on a rock, a blue one dangled from a bush. His eyes slowly swept the area. Orange— lavender—white—but where was the pink one? He looked more carefully. There it was, crumpled on the grass near a fallen log! Cowherd dashed out, grabbed the pink gown, and darted back to his hiding place. Unfortunately, in his hurry he stepped on a brittle twig. The fairies, about to leave the water, were alarmed by the crackling sound. In a twinkling they put on their clothes and flew away. That is, all except Weaving Maid.

Weaving Maid stood on the shore, her heart gripped by panic. She called after her sisters, "I cannot find my gown. Come back and help me look for it. Do not leave me here alone." But the fairies were already out of sight, veiled by a bank of gathering clouds.

Weaving Maid did not know what to do. She could not fly home unclothed, and to add to her discomfort, the brisk morning air made her shiver.

With Weaving Maid's pink gown draped over his arm, Cow- herd stepped into the open where she could see him. Frightened by his sudden appearance, she darted into a clump of tall reeds.

"Have no fear," Cowherd called after her. "I promise to return your gown if you will but listen to what I must tell you." Weaving Maid peeked warily at Cowherd. In his quiet, comfort- ing way, he was able to convince her that he meant no harm, and she grew less fearful. Too timid to speak, she merely nodded her head when he repeated his promise, whereupon Cowherd gave her the gown.

Clothed in her fairy robe, jet black hair touching her shoul- ders, she was the most dazzling creature Cowherd had ever seen. His whole being was aquiver when she sat down beside him.

"Last night," Cowherd explained, "my cow spoke to me. At first I did not believe my ears, but her words were unmistakably clear." Weaving Maid listened, entranced, as Cowherd recount- ed, step by step, the instructions he was to follow. "I did exactly

Cowherd grabbed the pink gown and darted back to his hiding place.

as I was told,'' he concluded, ''but I could not bear to watch you trembling in the cold. Therefore, I returned your gown before receiving your promise to marry me. Now I ask you, Weaving Maid, will you consent to be my wife?''

Weaving Maid was secretly pleased when Cowherd proposed marriage. This handsome, mild-mannered young man had aroused her tender feelings. The idea of remaining on earth as his wife appealed to her. Yet she had some lingering misgivings. Would her fairy grandmother agree to such a match? Familiar only with the ways of heaven, adapting to life on earth might be difficult for her. But Weaving Maid had fallen in love with Cowherd, and she made her decision. She lowered her eyes and her words were soft and sweet.

''Yes, I will be your wife,'' she said.

Cowherd was elated. He could not believe his good fortune. ''I will care for you always,'' he promised. ''To make you happy will be my only desire.''

Cowherd kept his promise. He worked even harder than before to please his adored wife. To his small house he added a roomy kitchen where Weaving Maid had space enough to set up her loom. Her skill at the art of weaving was unsurpassed, and her exquisite tapestries were snapped up at high prices in the marketplace. Their happiness overflowed when they became parents, first of a son, and later, of a daughter. The bright boy learned early from his father how to help with the daily tasks. The affectionate little daughter brightened their home with her sunny nature.

On a summer evening, Weaving Maid, Cowherd, and the children were resting in the garden. They watched the full moon rise and shed its comforting light over the earth. Their little daughter pointed to the sky. ''There is the first star,'' she cried. ''See how pretty it is!''

A sudden stab of fear touched Weaving Maid's heart. She rarely thought of her former life, for she was so content here on earth, surrounded by her loving family. But she could not rid herself of the apprehension that sometimes beset her. She truly belonged to heaven, and if, someday, she were summoned to return, how could she explain it to her children? Weaving Maid decided then and there to prepare them for the truth which they would inevitably learn. She would tell them of her past.

"My dear children, tonight, as the stars appear one by one in the night sky, I feel I must reveal to you a secret I have kept for many years. I have not always had an earthly existence. It is only since I married your father that I have dwelt on earth. I was born the youngest granddaughter of the Emperor of Heaven, and the Fairy Mother Goddess is my grandmother. From the time I was a little girl she taught me how to spin the clouds, to weave the constellations from the stars, to fashion the archer, the dipper, and the bear." Weaving Maid recalled wistfully the pleasant memories of her youth.

"Mother," her son asked in childish wonder, "do you miss your home in heaven?"

"Oh, no," Weaving Maid reassured him. "You and your sister and your father are very dear to me, and I would never choose to leave you. But sometimes I worry that my fairy grandmother does not know where I am and may be looking for me. I pray that she will not be angry if she discovers that I reside here on earth. Then she might force me to return to heaven with her, and that would break my heart."

The children put their arms around their mother. "We will not let you go," they said, with the confidence only the very young can muster. "Your grandmother will not take you away. You will remain with us forever." Weaving Maid hugged them and smiled, allaying their fears, while she herself remained troubled.

Cowherd was feeding his cow one day when he realized she was becoming old and feeble. Her rump was thin and bony, and she limped when she walked. He knew that her days were drawing to a close. When he patted her head she looked at him mournfully.

"What ails you, my dear friend?" he asked her, though he did not expect a reply. To his amazement the cow spoke as she had once before.

"You are a good master," she said in a weak, shaky voice, "and I am grateful for the many years you have treated me so well. Now my time on earth is over. I am speaking to you for the very last time. Again, I ask you to follow my instructions. When I have breathed my last breath, do not bury me until you have removed my entire skin. Scrape it clean and tan it. When the skin becomes soft and pliable, store it in a safe place. There may come a time when you are in great need. If you are faced with danger, wrap yourself in my skin and I will do my best to help you." Two days later the cow was dead.

Cowherd and Weaving Maid grieved over her loss, and the children were inconsolable. Following her instructions exactly as she had given them, Cowherd prepared her skin and stored it away.

The time scale in heaven is different from the time scale on earth. Several years in the human world are equivalent to only a few days of celestial time.

At first the Fairy Mother Goddess did not miss her granddaughter, for she had many duties to perform. It was she who had to darken the clouds to warn of an impending storm; it was she who, at sunset, painted the western sky. Not till the earth slept under a blanket of darkness did she cease her labors and rest.

The Fairy Mother Goddess learned of Weaving Maid's absence when she gathered her granddaughters together. She wished to grant them permission to return to earth and bathe again in the upper stream. Before she sent them off, it was her habit to count them.

"One of you is missing," she announced angrily. "Who is it that did not come immediately when I called?" She was enraged, for she could not abide disobedience.

Her granddaughters had known all along that Weaving Maid was not among them. They recalled how they had fled in panic and how they had ignored her pleas for help. Never had they mentioned it to a soul, but now one of them, more outgoing than the rest, spoke up.

"Grandmother," she lied, "we were unaware that Weaving Maid was not with us until we returned from our last earthly visit, but by then it was too late. We think she may have met with some misfortune and may still be on earth."

The Fairy Mother Goddess did not waste a moment. "I shall ask the God Fairy to accompany me. We will search for Weaving Maid and bring her back."

The evening meal was almost ready. The children were playing quietly at the table. Weaving Maid had just sat down to rest when, with a loud clatter, the door of her house blew open. It banged against the inside wall, shaking dust from the rafters. Weaving Maid whirled around and was confronted by the Fairy Mother Goddess and the God Fairy. Terrified by the sudden appearance of the strangers, the children clung to their mother and began to cry. Without a word, the two fairies tore Weaving Maid from their grasp and whisked her away between them. The frightened children saw their mother vanish from view.

When Cowherd returned home after the day's work, he found his son and daughter holding on to each other and weeping bitterly. Weaving Maid was nowhere to be seen. "Where is your mother?" he asked the children.

Between sobs they told him that their mother had been taken away by two fairies. "Will Mother return, will we ever see her again?" they whimpered, and they ran to their father for comfort.

Cowherd gathered them in his arms and held them close. "We will find her. I will think of a way."

Cowherd was confused and overcome by a feeling of helplessness. His head cradled in his hands, he sat, unable to think. Then the memory of words almost forgotten flooded back into his mind. "There may come a time when you are in great need. Wrap yourself in my skin and I will do my best to help you."

Cowherd took the skin from its place of storage. He draped it over his back, tied the loose ends across his chest, pulled the upper end and the horns over his head, and let the tail stretch out behind him. He waited to see what would happen.

A peculiar sensation coursed through his body. He felt his feet begin to leave the ground. He knew at once he would be able to fly, but he was not yet ready. He removed the skin and laid it on the table.

From a length of stout bamboo he fashioned a carrying pole. Then with leather thongs he tied two of Weaving Maid's largest straw baskets securely to either end. He lifted the children gently and lowered them into the baskets. After drawing the magic skin over his head, he balanced the pole across his back and stepped out the door.

Cowherd felt himself rise into the air, and soon he and the children were lifted higher and higher above the earth. The hope of a reunion with Weaving Maid filled him with joyful expectation, but his buoyant mood was soon replaced by apprehension.

One by one the stars disappeared. The moon hid herself behind dark clouds. A strong wind came up and whipped the baskets round and round. It was all Cowherd could do just to keep the pole steady. Icy hailstones pelted down about them and the children cried out in fear. Cowherd had to shout to be heard. "This will soon be over," he reassured them. Without a star to steer by, Cowherd felt that they were suspended in an empty, endless void. All at once he felt a tug, then a push. It was undeniable; they were being propelled forward on a steady course. The magic of the cow's skin had once again come to their rescue. They were safe.

By the time the storm abated, Cowherd was close to the abode of the Fairy Mother Goddess. He felt lightheaded with renewed hope, but he had not reckoned with her powerful wizardry. She

Interlocking their wings, the magpies formed a bridge across the silver river.

could see long distances, even through clouds and mist, and she knew that Cowherd and his children were about to invade her heavenly domain. She called forth her strongest soldiers. They stood in a solid line, their lances raised in battle position. Two of them, the fiercest-looking of all, were holding Weaving Maid by her shoulders. When she saw Cowherd and the children coming closer, she tried to free herself from their grip. Strain as she might, she could not take the smallest step.

The Fairy Mother Goddess pulled out one of her jade hairpins. Waving it through the air she created a silver river, whose waters shimmered with the reflections of a million stars. Cowherd and the children were cut off from Weaving Maid and stood forlornly on one side, while she called pitifully to them from the other.

A flock of magpies, bedecked in their sleek black and white plumage, witnessed the unfolding of the hapless events. Their sympathy went out to Cowherd and his children. Behind their leader they flew in close formation, interlocking their wings to form a bridge that spanned the silver river. Then they beckoned Cowherd and the children to pass over it.

The instant they stepped on the bridge, Weaving Maid tore herself away from the soldiers' grip and ran toward her family. Halfway across, they met and embraced, laughing and crying at the same time. Even the Fairy Mother Goddess was moved by their love for one another, and it softened her heart.

"Your earthly family will be granted permission to reside in heaven," she promised Weaving Maid, "but they must make their home far from the Fairy Kingdom. Each year, on the seventh day of the seventh month, I shall permit them to visit you."

On a clear night if there is not a hint of haze in the sky, you will see two stars, brighter than all the rest, winking at each other from opposite sides of the Milky Way. Watch them for a while, and if you are lucky you may see them moving closer and closer together. But only on the seventh day of the seventh month.

Meng-
Jiang
Nyu

The good neighbors, Meng and Jiang, lived at the edge of a small village surrounded by rich green rice paddies. Their roughly built cottages stood close together, separated only by a crude, latticed fence. With their wives toiling beside them, they planted, hoed, weeded, and in the fall, harvested their meager crops. For the most part, their lives were tranquil. Thus, accustomed to the slow, unchanging pattern of daily existence, they were quite unprepared for the wondrous thing that happened to them.

One day Meng dropped a watermelon seed behind his cottage. It germinated and sent forth a sturdy vine that crept along the ground, sending out curly tendrils. It climbed over the fence and finally came to rest near Jiang's kitchen door. All through the summer months the vine produced a myriad of golden blossoms. Disappointingly, it bore only a single melon. But what a fine specimen it was! Large and plump, without a blemish to mar its smooth, glossy skin, it ripened to perfection.

Now Meng and Jiang had to decide who was its rightful owner.

"The fruit grew on your side of the fence, and therefore it belongs to you," Meng offered graciously. "I shall be most happy if you find it as delicious to the taste as it is pleasing to the eye."

"No, no," countered Jiang. "The roots from which it drew nourishment were in your yard. Surely, my dear friend, in all fairness it belongs to you."

In the end, they and their wives decided to share it. Jiang carried the heavy, ripe melon into his house and placed it on the table. The others gathered round to watch him make the first cut through the green rind. As the knife sliced deeper into the flesh, the melon fell apart into two perfect halves, revealing a most astonishing sight. Instead of juicy pink pulp and shiny black seeds, they found a tiny baby girl, perfectly formed from head to toe, smiling up at them. They were struck dumb with surprise.

"This is a gift from heaven," declared Meng when he had regained his voice. "Neither you, good friends, nor we, have been blessed with a child. Together we would have shared the melon; together let us care for this little one and raise her as our own."

They named the infant Meng-Jiang Nyu, daughter of both the Meng and the Jiang families. With two mothers and two fathers, Meng-Jiang Nyu received a double portion of love and affection throughout her happy childhood. As the years passed, she grew into a comely maiden whose hand was sought by many suitors.

Meng-Jiang Nyu was eighteen on the day of her marriage to Wan Chi-liang. Everyone delighted in the lovely couple. She, dainty as a flower in her red wedding dress, glowed with happiness. And Chi-liang in his new, belted tunic was a handsome groom. The entire village was invited to witness the ceremony and partake of the feast that lasted for several days. The festivities over, the young bride and groom settled down to the routines of village life. They thought of themselves as truly fortunate, for they never felt hunger nor suffered from the cold. Deeply in love with his wife, Chi-liang found pleasure in fulfilling her every wish.

Their peaceful life was shattered one late summer day. Barely moments after they had come in from the fields, a stranger appeared at their door. He was dressed in an official's gown, and behind him stood two men in army uniform. With no word of explanation, he commanded his soldiers to seize Chi-liang and take him outside. Meng-Jiang Nyu, a look of bewilderment on her face, watched them push her husband toward the milling crowd assembled in the center of the village road.

The younger men from the neighboring cottages had all been rounded up, and they stood in a tight knot ringed by armed guards. Women, children, and older people had been ordered to remain at some distance.

Meng-Jiang Nyu's pounding heart made it difficult for her to breathe. As she approached the villagers, she heard a woman ask, "Could the emperor be conscripting men again? How well I remember when they took my father. I was just a young girl. I never saw him again."

Grandfather Hu, a village elder who was respected by all, offered his opinion. "The emperor has probably been convinced by his advisers to undertake another one of his foolish projects. No good can come of this."

Children fidgeted and cried, while the restlessness of the by-standers increased as their anxiety mounted.

"Silence!" shouted the official. "I bring an order from the emperor." The murmuring ceased. "Wild horsemen are attacking from the north. These barbarians are looting and killing, burning whole villages to the ground. The emperor has issued a call for all able-bodied men to build a great wall, the highest and thickest wall ever built by men. The enemy will never be able to break through its impenetrable defense, and our people will be able to live in peace. It is the duty of every man to obey the emperor's summons. Anyone who refuses does so on pain of death."

"Forward!" he commanded. Lined up three abreast, the men were marched off. Soldiers carrying spears walked along the sides of the column. Escape was impossible.

Tearful parents, wives, and children were left behind to fend for themselves. An old farmer leaning on a cane shook his head sadly.

"Heaven alone knows if I shall ever see my son before my life is over," he said in a hoarse whisper.

Only a few months had passed since that terrifying day, but for Meng-Jiang Nyu it seemed like ages. Without her husband at her side, time dragged interminably. In her fervent prayers she asked that he be kept from hunger and thirst. The winter would bring its bitter winds that blow unceasingly from the mountains. How was Chi-liang going to survive in so hostile a climate without a warm jacket and cotton quilted shoes?

The last days of autumn were drawing to an end. It was the time of year when the dusk came early, but Meng-Jiang Nyu would not stop until darkness forced her to lay aside her sewing. Her needle flew ever faster as she layered fabric with cotton padding, fashioning a comfortable outer garment. She took particular care to design thick-soled shoes, sewing them with extra strong thread. Time was her enemy as she worked to finish the task she had set for herself.

Meng-Jiang Nyu swore a solemn oath. Chi-liang would not do without winter clothes. This she vowed. No matter how perilous the journey, she would take them to him herself. A woman traveling alone might encounter unexpected dangers, and she wondered if she would endure the long trek on foot. But she banished the troubling thoughts from her mind.

The evening before her departure, she prepared a small bag of rice and another of millet, only the barest necessities to sustain her along the way. On a large cloth square she placed Chi-liang's jacket and shoes. By tying the opposite corners of the square together, she made a bundle to carry over her arm.

Before daybreak she left her home. No one was yet awake, and the narrow streets of the village were deserted. It was still quite dark. In the east, Meng-Jiang Nyu saw a rosy glow that announced the beginning of a new day. "A good omen," she mused.

Word had come back to the village that the section of the wall where Chi-liang was working lay at a great distance. If the snows came early, there was no telling how long it would take to get there. Meng-Jiang Nyu had learned that she must travel in a northwesterly direction, but beyond that she did not even know for certain where she would find her husband.

Never having traveled more than a few miles from her village, she could not imagine the vastness that lay beyond it. Nor could she conceive, in her wildest flight of fancy, the size and length of the wall that the emperor had planned. Neither could she picture a wall three thousand miles long that would climb over high mountains, descend into deep valleys, and cross forbidding deserts. But the grandeur of the emperor's ambitious undertaking meant nothing to her. She only knew she must plod ahead for as long as it would take her to join Chi-liang.

As the days wore on, Meng-Jiang Nyu found she had to rest more and more frequently. Often, as she passed through little villages, she begged for food. She had finished her rice and millet long ago. People who spoke to her and learned where she was bound praised her devotion but shook their heads in disbelief.

Once she heard a woman lamenting loudly to a friend, "Our sons are gone, our daughters widowed, and the pile of dead grows ever larger at the foot of the emperor's great wall." Meng-Jiang Nyu shuddered.

From sunrise to sunset she doggedly trudged on. When darkness fell, she looked for a place to lay her head. Many a night her bed was just a pile of scratchy straw.

The day Meng-Jiang Nyu reached the Yellow River, her strength was beginning to fail. At the point where she stood, the river was wide and the current of its silt-laden water, swift. For the peasants who lived along its banks it was life-sustaining, but for Meng-Jiang Nyu it was yet another obstacle that had to be overcome. Except for a lone shepherd grazing his flock of sheep, there was not a soul in sight.

Meng-Jiang Nyu reached the Yellow River.

"I have not come this far in vain," she thought. "I will not turn back!"

With determination born of despair, she walked into the water holding Chi-liang's clothes over her head to keep them dry. A few yards out from the shore her feet could no longer touch bottom, and she tried to swim. The effort to keep afloat was beyond her endurance. Finally she gave up the struggle and let the river claim her. The cold water dragged her toward the murky bottom— down, down into an inky blackness.

Meng-Jiang Nyu's distress did not go unnoticed. A river god came to her rescue, plucking her from the deep and carrying her to the opposite shore.

When Meng-Jiang Nyu opened her eyes, a shadowy specter was hovering over her.

"My brave child, do not abandon hope," it soothed. "All the spirits along the way will help you to the end of your journey." The shadow drifted away and melted into the air. Meng-Jiang Nyu was alone. She had no recollection of how she had reached the other side of the river. Nor was she sure she had heard the encouraging promise of help.

Wearily, she picked up her bundle. Everything was wet through. Before moving on she would have to wait for the clothes to dry. She wrung out Chi-liang's jacket and spread it on the ground. When she reached for his shoes, a miracle occurred. Spellbound, she saw the shoes turn into two blackbirds. From then on, never ceasing their shrill chatter, the blackbirds led her day after day in a northerly direction. Whenever she tired, they alighted on the ground near her and waited until she had regained her strength. At night they roosted in a nearby tree while she slept. One morning, Meng-Jiang Nyu awoke, trembling with cold. Her fingers and toes were numb and she ached all over. Reaching to pick up her bundle, she was surprised to see Chi-liang's shoes standing neatly, side by side. The blackbirds, her guides and constant companions, were gone. They had fulfilled their mission, for they had led Meng-Jiang Nyu close to her destination.

Meng-Jiang Nyu dragged her swollen, painful feet along a dusty road. At first the road was flat; then it began to climb steeply. When she reached high ground, her eyes took in an incredible scene. The figures she saw moving about resembled a scurrying swarm of ants. She quickened her pace. Now she could see more clearly. Files of men, backs bent under the weight of heavy stones, were struggling to the top of the unfinished wall. Others were lugging buckets of mortar to fill the spaces between the rocks. Covered from head to foot by the dry, brown sand, they were indistinguishable, one from the other. How could she ever find Chi-liang among that multitude?

With unaccustomed boldness, she approached a small group of men who were attempting to warm their hands over a smoldering fire. Timidly she explained, "I am looking for my husband. He is called Chi-liang." She told them the name of their village and the day on which he was conscripted, but they only looked at her with pity.

"I am sorry I cannot help you," said one of the men. "This wall has no beginning and no end. The wind batters us, the white snow blinds us, we have little food and no warm clothing. There is only toil without rest. Every day we see good comrades fall, and many more will die of exhaustion. Hundreds are already buried inside the wall. We admire your loyalty to your husband, but you should not endanger your own life trying to do the impossible. Better that you return home. You will never find him."

But Meng-Jiang Nyu could not be discouraged. Bravely she continued to search. Wherever she went she asked for Chi-liang. The relentless wind tore at her clothing, her face and hands became rough and red from exposure. She ate very little and slept hardly a wink. At last, fatigue conquered her, and Meng-Jiang Nyu fell asleep on the frozen ground. She did not know how much time had passed before she became aware of someone

prodding her. ''You must not lie here or you will freeze to death,''
a man warned.

Shaking uncontrollably, she managed to say, ''I am looking for
my husband. He bears the name Chi-liang.'' Once again, she
recited the name of their village and the date on which he was
taken.

''Yes, I knew your husband,'' the stranger responded. ''I remember him well. We were assigned the task of making bricks
and he was the best worker in the section. It pains me to tell you
that we found him one morning covered by newly fallen snow,
lifeless. With many others he lies buried within the wall.''

Meng-Jiang Nyu could not hold back the flood of salty tears
that stung her cold cheeks. She blamed herself for Chi-liang's
death. She had come too late to save him.

''How can it be that so gentle a husband has perished so young?
The Great Wall takes more lives than the plundering enemy.''

A wife's devotion can sometimes move mountains. Wailing
bitterly, Meng-Jiang Nyu cried out to heaven. The sun vanished
behind threatening clouds. A violent tempest churned up the
powdery sand, and rain fell in icy sheets. Bolts of lightning
streaked through the sky. With a deafening clap of thunder, a
section of the wall collapsed, bricks and stones spilling out together with human bones and skulls.

''Do not be alarmed, brave wife of Chi-liang. Heaven has
witnessed your sorrow. You will seek out your husband's bones
from among all the others.'' The words were sharp and clear, but
there was not a soul in sight. Meng-Jiang Nyu stood transfixed
amid the pile of rubble.

''But how will I know which among the many are his?''

''Have no fear. You will succeed, for when love is sincere and
true, two people become as one. They share thoughts, hopes,
feelings. Their blood, their bones, their very tissues mingle. Do
not despair, you will find a way.''

''Alas,'' moaned Meng-Jiang Nyu. ''In this jumble lying here,

A section of The Great Wall collapsed.

strewn this way and that, are the bones of Chi-liang. Oh mountains, hills, desert of yellow sands,'' she pleaded, ''favor me, and give me a sign that I may recognize those that belong to him. I cannot choose for I cannot tell one from another.'' Unaware of what she was doing, she bit down on her thumb until she drew blood. She watched a drop fall upon a bone, slide off the surface, and reach the ground. Suddenly the words she had just heard took on meaning.

''If the bones are Chi-liang's, my blood will mingle with his and sink into them. If the bones belong to others, the blood will remain apart.''

This time, with determination, she bit down harder and then shook her hand, spattering the blood about. What she hoped for did not happen. Again, and still again, she tried. Each time her blood slid quickly off the bones. ''One last time,'' she told herself. Though the pain brought tears to her eyes, she bit down with all her might. The blood flowed freely and she flung it as far and as wide as she could. One quivering red dot landed on a bone lying apart from the others. At once the blood sank into its chalky whiteness. This bone must belong to Chi-liang. Of this she was certain. Feverishly she continued to search, and soon she recovered the rest. Chi-liang's bones would receive a proper burial, and his soul would not have to wander aimlessly in search of peace.

Laden with the heavy blow fate had dealt her, Meng-Jiang Nyu turned to the south and began her sad journey homeward.

Ma Liang and His Magic Brush

Even before Ma Liang reached his tenth birthday he was carrying upon his frail, boyish shoulders the burdens of a grown man. After his mother and father were taken in the year of the great tidal wave, he was left all alone in the world. To earn a few coins he toiled endless hours, chopping wood or cutting weeds for his neighbors. The villagers, poor themselves, paid him only a pittance for his labors, just enough to provide a bowl of rice for a single meal each day. His flimsy hut stood close to the sandy beach. With its leaky roof and splintered door, it afforded him scanty protection against the elements.

Though deprived of the simplest comforts of life, Ma Liang still found moments of pleasure. Ambling along the shell-strewn shore, he was fascinated when a gray-and-white gull suddenly swooped down from the sky to catch an unsuspecting fish. He noticed the shape of its wings as it dipped and turned, the angle of its tail, the grace with which it skimmed over the water.

Often he entertained himself by using a broken twig to draw birds in the moist sand. If he were lucky enough to find a piece of charcoal, he would search for a smooth stone and cover it with images of animals or flowers. Before long, Ma Liang was drawing with ease anything within sight of his keen, observing eyes.

Day by day his sketches became ever more lifelike. While gathering firewood on a mountainside he found a large, flat stone. Upon it he drew a newborn chick, complete in every detail from its fuzzy head to its spindly legs. It looked so real an eagle soared overhead ready to pounce down and carry it off. On a barefaced rocky hillside, he drew a wolf poised to attack. Sheep and cows grazing on the tender grass fled to another meadow.

There was no doubt that Ma Liang possessed a great talent. But a pointed twig and a sharp stone were poor tools for an artist. Ma Liang desperately yearned to have a brush. He imagined the magnificent landscapes he would paint, peaked mountains with a high waterfall splashing into a pool below, or a broad sailing ship moving majestically in the water.

Each week Ma Liang dutifully delivered firewood to a famous scholar. Arriving with his bundle of sticks one day, he saw an artist engaged in painting a portrait of the elderly sage. For several minutes Ma Liang watched, fascinated by the movements of the artist's brush. Ma Liang approached the artist and courteously made his plea. "Kind sir, how I dream of becoming an artist like you! But I am so poor I do not have the money for a brush. Please, sir, since you have so many to choose from, would you lend me just one until I can save enough to buy my own?"

The busy artist glared at him and said scornfully, "You, an ignorant peasant boy, aspire to paint like me? What a ridiculous idea! Go away and do not interrupt me while I am working."

Ma Liang placed the firewood in its proper corner, received a few coins and left, disheartened.

One summer evening after long hours of toil, Ma Liang returned home and fell asleep on the beach under a canopy of stars. Beneath the white moon stretched the silvery sea. Out of the undulating wavelets a fountain erupted, spewing upwards a shower of glistening droplets. From within the spray arose a curious apparition. The dripping figure, seaweed clinging to his long white beard, glided effortlessly toward the shore. In his hand he held a slender, shiny object.

"Ma Liang," whispered the strange old man, "take this magic brush. In it dwells a mighty spirit. If used to help others, it will bring joy and prosperity. If used unwisely, it will bring disaster.'' Having spoken, the weird figure disappeared into the sea as mysteriously as he had come.

Ma Liang awoke with a feeling of elation. His momentary happiness faded, however, when he realized that he had only been dreaming. He started to pick himself up off the ground when he became aware of a weight in his right hand. Glancing down, he saw that his fingers were clutching a brush. ''Perhaps I am not yet awake.'' He shook his head and blinked his eyes.

Ma Liang examined the brush closely. The handle was made of the finest ivory; the tip, of sable hairs.

Glowing with excitement, Ma Liang ran along the beach shouting, ''It's true! I have a paintbrush at last!''

Looking for a place to try out his newly acquired gift, he came upon a piece of driftwood. With a few deft strokes he drew a yellow-tailed perch. No sooner did he apply the last stroke when it came to life and flopped clumsily on the sand. Ma Liang grabbed the panting fish, waded into the shallow waves, and threw it into the water. He was relieved to see it swim away.

Next, he drew a cormorant. When the long-necked bird flew out over the sea, Ma Liang knew he possessed an uncommon treasure. ''My brush will be used to perform only good deeds,'' he vowed.

Stopping at each house in his little village, carrying his brush and a roll of cotton paper, he would ask his neighbors how he could benefit them.

''My nets are worn and full of holes,'' complained a fisherman. ''How shall I feed my family?'' Just a few criss-cross lines with his brush and Ma Liang replaced the old net with a strong new one.

A peasant came, wringing his hands and crying, ''My well has run dry.'' With his magic brush, Ma Liang caused a well to materialize, complete with bucket and rope. The peasant drank the cool water and rejoiced.

Soon the villagers came to depend upon Ma Liang to help them whenever they were in distress. One had an empty grain bin, another a threadbare shirt, a third a broken plow. For each, Ma Liang provided according to his needs. In return, he was regarded by all with warmth and affection.

News of Ma Liang's magic brush was carried to an adjacent village where there lived a wealthy landlord. Immediately, he sent for Ma Liang. Visions of gold and silver danced in the landlord's head.

"I shall be the richest man on earth," he crowed.

When Ma Liang was brought before him, the landlord wasted no time in pleasantries.

"Paint a casket of gold pieces," he commanded. Ma Liang was shocked by the man's avarice.

"I cannot do that, sir. My brush serves only those who are in need. You, Master, want for nothing and already possess more wealth than most."

The landlord flew into a rage. "Lock him in the stable," he shouted to his servants, "and give him neither food nor water. He'll soon change his mind when his stomach is empty and his mouth, dry."

The howling wind whistled through the open slats of the empty stable. Ma Liang shivered in the penetrating cold. Though his fingers were stiff, he managed to paint a large stove. Then he added logs to burn and tasty cakes to eat. Soon he was warm and snug.

The landlord was served his supper and ate heartily. He rose from the table and walked toward the window. Outside, the temperature had dropped to below freezing and thick flakes of snow whirled through the air. It was a good night to be indoors in his well-heated house.

About to turn away from the window, the landlord noticed a light burning in the stable. Grumbling that he would have to venture out in the storm, he, nevertheless, decided to investigate.

He wrapped himself in his fur-lined robe, pulled on his knee-length boots, and clumped toward the stable in the deep snow. Through a slit in the wall he saw a large stove in which burned a crackling fire. Ma Liang, his feet propped up against it, was enjoying a piece of cake. Furious, the landlord summoned his two servants to come quickly.

"We will teach that boy a lesson he will never forget. Give him a good thrashing," he roared, "and take his brush away."

When the servants swung open the stable door, Ma Liang was gone. They saw only a ladder leaning against the eastern wall. "After him, after him!" the landlord raged. By the time the servants had scrambled up the ladder, Ma Liang was galloping away on a magnificent steed, holding aloft a burning torch to light his way. With the aid of his magic brush, Ma Liang had made a clean escape.

"The boy has gotten away," the servants reported, but the landlord refused to rely on their word. He insisted on climbing the ladder to see for himself. As soon as he reached the topmost rung, the ladder collapsed under his weight, sending him crashing to the ground. The servants had to help him to his feet, and they led him sputtering and embarrassed back to the house.

Ma Liang was now safely out of harm's reach. "I was able to shake off the grasping landlord," he reasoned, "but others just like him will ask for special favors and punish me if I refuse their selfish demands. I must leave my own village and travel afar to a place where no one has heard of Ma Liang and his magic brush."

For several days Ma Liang journeyed through the countryside until he reached a bustling city. At first it was difficult to find lodgings, but with perseverance, he was able to rent a room in the home of a local merchant.

Equipped with a small wooden box to serve as a table and a short stool to sit upon, he would arrive in the marketplace early each morning, unroll his paper and begin to paint. Crowds gathered round to admire his remarkable skill. In each drawing he deliberately left out one minor detail, for Ma Liang was determined never again to allow his pictures to come alive.

It was on a warm spring day that the unexpected happened. The throngs in the marketplace were unusually large, and Ma Liang was surrounded on all sides by curious onlookers. He had just drawn a perfect likeness of a stately crane. While waiting for the painting to dry, he busied himself cleaning the bristles of his brush. Someone accidentally nudged his arm, causing a single drop of black ink to land precisely in the eye of the snow-white crane, the eye that Ma Liang had purposely left blank. The painting was complete! Flapping its wings noisily, the great bird rose and flew above the heads of the stunned bystanders. In wonderment, they followed its course until it became a tiny speck in the sky. Ma Liang snatched up his stool and raced away, never stopping until he was back in his room.

From mouth to mouth the tale of the boy with the magic paintbrush spread through the city and beyond. Eventually it reached the royal palace. A guard told a soldier who told a general who told a courtier who told the emperor.

Straightaway, the emperor assigned two soldiers to look for Ma Liang. To his instructions he added a dire threat. "Do not return without the boy or you may lose your heads!"

The emperor reigned over his subjects with an iron fist. He had earned neither their love nor their respect, for he was a selfish, imperious man who had little regard for their welfare. Even now, as he awaited Ma Liang's arrival, he rubbed his palms together with satisfaction. Ma Liang would provide him with fabulous riches. He would be the most powerful emperor in all the world.

Before Ma Liang was escorted into the throne room, a table had been prepared on orders from the emperor. On it, neatly laid out, were pots of paint, and paper scrolls of the highest quality.

"Begin at once," the emperor directed. "Paint a dragon and color him scarlet and gold. When he comes to life he will bring me good luck."

The bird rose above the heads of the stunned bystanders.

But Ma Liang did not paint a dragon. Instead, so quickly that the emperor barely noticed the movement of the brush, he painted an enormous snake. The ugly serpent crawled off the table and slithered toward the emperor.

"Get it away from me," cried the emperor, shrinking back in dread. His obedient servants beat the snake until it lay lifeless at the emperor's feet. Still the emperor was not deterred. Hiding his anger behind a false smile, he spoke in a honeyed voice. "Ma Liang, I beg you, paint the bird that brings happiness—paint a phoenix."

Ma Liang worked speedily, turning out, with just a few dabs of ink, a sleek, black crow. It rose to the ceiling, cawing raucously. Before the servants could catch it, several porcelain vases were shattered, the carpet soiled, and the emperor's golden throne bespattered.

Incensed, the emperor snatched the brush from Ma Liang's hand, and had him imprisoned in a dungeon below the palace.

"I shall try this magic myself," declared the emperor. Holding the brush awkwardly, he drew a ruby. The gem slid from the paper to the table. He felt its hardness and delighted in its blood-red color. The emperor was encouraged. He drew an emerald and marvelled at its delicate transparency.

"The magic brush works for me, too!" The emperor beamed with pleasure. He drew sapphires, diamonds, silver and gold nuggets, never stopping until he stood ankle deep in precious stones. The furious activity tired him, but when he tried to rest, the magic brush tugged at his arm and kept right on painting. His fingers stuck to the handle and he could not loosen them. By the time the emperor had filled the last inch of paper, he had amassed a mountain of jewels.

"If I had more paper, I could keep painting forever," he boasted. No sooner had the words escaped his lips when the mountain collapsed around him. His servants dug furiously and pulled him to safety, or he most surely would have been smothered.

The narrow escape sobered the emperor. He understood that only Ma Liang could control the magic brush. "Free the boy and bring him before me," he told the jailer.

The emperor tried to sound contrite when he spoke to Ma Liang. "I apologize, Ma Liang, for being so selfish and greedy. Now I understand that your brush must only be used to create beauty and goodness. Would you paint a restful scene for me, one that will soothe my inner being?"

On a large empty wall, Ma Liang drew a boundless blue sea under an azure sky. Despite this idyllic setting, the emperor could not suppress his greed. "Ah, Ma Liang," he sighed, "if only I could have a tree of gold."

Without replying, Ma Liang drew an island far out on the rolling waters. The emperor's temper was beginning to rise but he controlled his anger. "But I asked for a tree of gold," he complained meekly.

"You shall have it," Ma Liang assured him. The brush moved swiftly, and on the island appeared a tall tree, each branch entwined with golden filigree. The emperor waved his arms and danced for joy.

"Perfect, perfect, Ma Liang, but how can I reach the island?"

"I shall provide a splendid ship with masts and strong square sails," Ma Liang graciously offered. "I shall, for your pleasure, add a gangplank so you and your guards may embark."

"I have always enjoyed a sea voyage," said the emperor, smiling broadly, and he invited his guards to join him on board. The guards lifted the anchor; the ship rocked gently.

"How are we to set sail," the emperor called, "without a breeze?"

Ma Liang added several strokes. A soft wind filled the sails and the ship began to move.

"Faster," shouted the emperor. "At this pace, we shall never get there."

Ma Liang painted furiously. The wind took on the force of a

Ma Liang painted furiously.

gale, and water swept over the deck causing the ship to heel dangerously. The waves grew into rolling swells. The vessel floundered, nearly throwing its passengers overboard.

"Ma Liang, stop the wind," implored the emperor, panic-stricken. "Whatever you desire, I shall grant; only do not let us perish."

With a single stroke, Ma Liang wiped out the entire picture, leaving a blank wall. The emperor found himself sitting in a pool of water, quite alone and confused. "Where is Ma Liang?" he asked aloud.

To this day no one knows what happened to Ma Liang. He never returned to his village, nor has he been seen these many years. For all we know, he may still be wandering from place to place helping those in need with his magic brush.

From
the Year
of
the Rat
to
the Year
of
the Pig

Many centuries ago, the Chinese people judged the passing of time by the rhythms of the seasons. Warm breezes heralded the coming of spring and the time to plant; lasting sunlight and endless heat signaled summer's arrival; bountiful harvests were the prelude to the short, dreary days of winter. When the light of each day lengthened, they knew another cycle had begun.

The uncounted years rolled by until a time came when the people asked each other, "How are we to remember the important events that have occurred in our lives?" They could not recall when their sons and daughters had been born, or when their ancestors had died. They could not remember the great earthquake that had devastated their villages, or the terrible flood that had carried away thousands unable to flee to higher ground. They could make no records of the great famines that had taken a bitter toll of innocent lives, or the times when nature had been so bountiful their rice baskets were filled to overflowing.

Clearly they needed help to solve this dilemma. From all points of the land learned men gathered in a great assembly. They discussed, reasoned, argued and debated. Finally, worn out by their lengthy deliberations without reaching agreement, they decided to petition the Jade Emperor for advice. He readily agreed to come to their aid, but told them he needed several days to mull over so weighty a problem.

Although the Jade Emperor spent hours in deep contemplation, he could not formulate a proper plan. As he sat on his heavenly throne looking down upon the earth, he watched the ox pulling his master's plow, the sheep grazing on the hillside, the rooster scratching for worms near the henhouse. An idea took shape in the Jade Emperor's mind. He would arrange a contest and request all the animals to participate.

Fleet-footed runners were dispatched to invite the animals to prepare for a race. It was to take place when the pear trees bloomed, an auspicious time, for it was then that the Jade Emperor celebrated his birthday. The rules to be followed were simple. Each contestant had to cross a wide river whose swift current presented a formidable challenge. The first twelve to reach the opposite shore would have their names assigned to the years in order of their arrival. As a further incentive, the animals were assured they would be remembered with gratitude forever after, and that a grand celebration in their honor would be staged at the beginning of each year.

This news caused much excitement in the animal kingdom. Large and small, each creature of field and forest started to think of ways to outrace the others.

The cat and the rat, who lived under the same roof, were close friends. They discussed their chances. "We two might just as well forget the whole thing," the rat said unhappily. "There is no way we can cross the river. We cannot swim such a long distance in deep water."

"Don't give up so easily," answered the more optimistic cat. "There may be a way. What if we talk to the ox? He will have no difficulty crossing the river, for he is a powerful swimmer. Moreover, he is good-natured, and I am certain he will agree to help us."

"Tell me more," said the rat. He had some reservations.

"It is simple. We will merely climb upon his broad back and he will carry us across." The rat perked up his little ears.

"We might win yet!" he cried, and his gloomy countenance vanished.

Without delay, the two friends called on the ox. They told him that of all the animals, they liked him best. They praised him for his great size; they admired his curved horns. But most of all, they complimented him for his exceptional ability as a swimmer. The ox, whose brain was far smaller than his belly, was flattered.

"I would very much like to repay your kindness in some way," the naive ox offered, whereupon the cat and rat laid out their scheme. "You are most welcome to ride on my back," the ox assured them. "Since you both weigh so little, you will not be a burden to me."

On the day of the race, even before daybreak, the ox appeared on their doorstep. He had to wake them out of their slumber.

"Good morning, my good fellows," he greeted them cheerfully. "It's time to leave now." The rat was instantly alert, but the cat, still drowsy, stretched her lithe body and blinked. The impatient ox pawed the ground, anxious to get started.

"Make haste," he begged, "or we shall be late." With one leap, the cat was on the ox's back, while the rat scrambled up the side of the huge beast as best he could. Snorting and panting, the ox lumbered toward the river and stepped cautiously into the water.

"Look at all the jagged rocks," he complained. "My body is so large it will be impossible for me to avoid them."

"Do not worry," the cat assured him. "My eyes are sharp. I shall watch from your shoulder and keep you out of harm's way."

Timidly, the ox moved forward. Swimming was not easy, for the current was strong, and the cat's constant warnings made it impossible for him to steer a straight course.

When they passed midstream, there were fewer obstacles. The ox was relieved, but the rat became tense.

"If we all reach the shore at the same time," he reasoned to himself, "the cat, who can run faster than I, will be the winner."

This he would not permit. Silently he positioned himself behind the cat and tapped her on the back. "Look there," he shouted in his high-pitched, squeaky voice, "a great fish is jumping out of the water." As the cat turned her head, the rat, with little effort, pushed her off the ox's rump into the river. He last saw her looking at him, incomprehension and fear in her eyes.

The rat glanced backward and scanned the river. Black and yellow stripes flashed in the water. The tiger was rapidly catching up.

"Faster, faster," the rat urged. "Every minute counts."

Blowing bubbles out of his nose with each wheezing breath, the ox exerted himself to the utmost of his strength. With a final burst of energy, straining every muscle, he reached the opposite shore and pulled himself up on the sandy beach.

No sooner had the ox set foot on dry land than the wily rat jumped to the ground in front of him. Caught unawares, the ox almost fell trying to avoid stepping on his ungrateful passenger. Within seconds, the rat was bowing before the emperor, who had set up court on the north side of the river. Accompanied by his attendants and a scribe, he awaited the arrival of the contestants.

"Congratulations," said the Jade Emperor. "You are the first to arrive at the finish line." Then he ordered his scribe to list the rat as number one. "You have certainly won a great victory," the emperor continued, while the rat grinned with pleasure. "I should like to know how you got here, since you can neither swim far nor run fast."

The rat pushed out his chest and beamed. "Your Majesty," he answered with unashamed boastfulness, "though I am small in size, I have a good brain. I enlisted the assistance of a gracious friend, and here he is."

The ox stood there, water dripping from his woolly coat and forming a pool at his feet.

The Jade Emperor addressed him. "Do sit down and rest. You are undoubtedly tired. I am happy to inform you that you have

The rat pushed the cat into the river.

made an honorable showing. My scribe will record you as number two.'' The absence of the cat puzzled the ox, but he was so elated to have won second place, he cast aside his concern and made no mention of her disappearance.

The tiger was next to arrive. Soaked and disheveled, a sorry sight to behold, he collapsed at the Jade Emperor's feet.

''Am I the first one?'' he asked, too exhausted to notice that the rat and the ox were already there.

''I regret to inform you,'' answered the Jade Emperor, ''that the rat and the ox arrived before you. With your reputation for fleetness, how is it you were so late?''

''I met with an unforeseen difficulty,'' explained the tiger. ''I was swimming strongly and making good headway when I got caught in the swift current. It carried me downstream, and in seconds I was off course. I tried to reverse my direction but was pulled into a whirling eddy that spun me round and round and dragged me downward until I thought I would surely drown. It was only after a fearful struggle that I freed myself and made it to safety.''

''Well,'' chided the rat, ''those who depend only on their physical strength are doomed to failure.'' The tiger was about to pounce on the impudent rodent, but the Jade Emperor raised his hand and asked for silence.

''Please, we will have no quarrels today.'' Turning to his scribe, he directed him to record the tiger as number three.

To his own delighted surprise, the rabbit earned fourth place. He had started to cross the river, hopping from one exposed stone to another. Finally he reached the last rock visible above the surface, and he was still far from shore. Fortunately, fate intervened in the form of a log that came floating by. He clung to it, paddling furiously with his forelegs until it washed up on the sand.

''Enter him as number four,'' ordered the Jade Emperor, and the scribe wrote in the rabbit's name.

On a gust of wind, in blew a long-tailed, scaly dragon, his eyes blazing red, his flared nostrils belching smoke.

"Oh my, I see that four others have arrived before me." The dragon was in high spirits.

"I expected you to get here sooner," said the Jade Emperor with some amusement. "After all, you can fly."

"I could not neglect my other duties, Your Majesty," explained the dragon. "The people who dwell beyond the high mountains have had no rain for many weeks. Their fields are parched, their animals dying. I had to take time to move the rain clouds in their direction. Furthermore, on my way over I noticed the rabbit struggling to cross the river on a log, and I stopped to raise a helpful breeze to blow him ashore."

When the dragon finished his story, the Jade Emperor was pleased. "I commend you for your consideration toward others. Such charitable acts deserve high praise. The kind dragon will be number five." The scribe picked up his brush and wrote.

With a clattering of hoofs, the horse made his appearance in the midst of a cloud of blinding dust. He shook his head, switched his tail smartly, and was about to approach the Jade Emperor when he suddenly reared back on his hind legs and let out a whinny like the blast of a trumpet. The snake had crawled out from between his feet and had startled him. In the instant it took the horse to regain his composure, the unruffled snake, weaving to the right and to the left, flicking his forked tongue in and out of his mouth, sped ahead. He was assigned sixth place, and it was duly recorded.

"What is my rank?" asked the horse, who had trotted up before the Jade Emperor, still a little shaky after his unnerving experience.

"I'm sorry you had such a scare," said the Jade Emperor, "but do not be angry with the snake. Unlike the rest of us, he can neither walk nor run nor fly. Since he must crawl on the ground, he is often hidden from view. I don't think he meant any harm. At any rate," continued the Jade Emperor, trying to console the horse, "you are the winner of the seventh place." The scribe made the appropriate entry.

The sheep, the monkey, and the rooster were an odd trio when they presented themselves at the finish line. The sheep had recently been shorn and looked naked. He was so comical with his large, curled horns sticking out of his bald head that the Jade Emperor could barely suppress a chuckle.

The monkey, as usual, played the clown. Rather than walking sedately up to the Jade Emperor, he jumped, sprang, clambered up a nearby tree, then hung dangerously by his tail. Watching his antics, the Jade Emperor laughed heartily.

Strutting with pride, the rooster displayed his iridescent feathers. He crowed raucously, shaking his head to show off his elegant comb.

The Jade Emperor addressed them. "How did the three of you manage to cross the river? Not one of you can swim."

The rooster took it upon himself to act as spokesman. "From my high perch I noticed a raft near the water's edge. I flew down and was about to push off when I saw the monkey and the sheep standing near the river, looking dejected. I invited them on board, and it was a good thing I did. The raft, caught in tall weeds, was difficult to free. The monkey pulled, the sheep pushed, I stirred up a few waves with my wings, and we were off."

"Quite clever, I must admit," said the Jade Emperor. He turned to the scribe. "Please inscribe the sheep, the monkey, and the rooster as the eighth, ninth, and tenth winners."

The Jade Emperor looked in the direction of the river, hoping to glimpse the last two contestants. Ah, there was the dog. Shivering in the cool air, he shook himself, spattering water in every direction. His tongue hung loosely from one side of his mouth as he loped toward the finish line.

"Why did you tarry so long?" the Jade Emperor wished to know. "You are one of the best swimmers, and I thought surely you would be one of the first arrivals."

"Perhaps I was foolish," admitted the dog, "but since I hadn't bathed in a long while, and since the water in the river was so clean, I stopped to give myself a good washing. That is the reason for my tardiness." The dog wagged his tail happily.

"Number eleven," announced the Jade Emperor, and the scribe made the proper notation.

It had been a long day and everyone was weary. The animals were hoping the contest would end before nightfall and they could all go home.

Was that a squeal they heard?

The disgruntled black pig came waddling along. "Here I am at last," he said with relief. "I thought I'd never get here. Before I reached the river, my stomach began to grumble. My hunger pangs became so severe I simply had to stop to forage for something to eat. For miles I walked and could find only a few nibbles. I'm so relieved to be in your company for I am dying of hunger. Is there anything to eat?"

The Jade Emperor shook his head. "Aren't you at all interested in finding out whether you have gained a place among the twelve winners of the contest?"

"To tell the truth, Your Majesty, when my stomach is empty I can't keep my mind on anything but a pail of juicy slops."

"Indeed," said the Jade Emperor, smiling, "I am pleased to inform you that you are number twelve." He motioned to the scribe to record the pig as the final winning contestant.

Majestically the Jade Emperor rose and surveyed the group of animals with satisfaction. They listened politely as he addressed them. "I thank you all for your splendid effort. The competition is over and each one of you will receive a medal of merit." He signaled to the scribe. "Bring the lacquered box to me and I shall distribute the awards while you call out the names in their proper order."

"The Year of the Rat." The scribe pronounced his words clearly and in a resounding voice. Wild applause broke out.

The cat lunged for the rat.

Each animal was honored in his turn to the sounds of loud cheering and clapping.

The ox lowed, the tiger leaped into the air, while the rabbit hopped up and down. The dragon belched fire, the snake hissed, the horse whinnied. The sheep, the monkey, and the rooster joined in, baa-ing, chattering, and crowing. When the dog added his bark and the pig her oink, the din became unbearable.

The Jade Emperor, gratified with the results of the contest, called for order. He was about to dismiss his animal friends when a sudden commotion was heard. Bedraggled, her wet, tousled fur standing on end, the cat sprang before the Jade Emperor. "Am I too late?" she asked breathlessly.

"I'm sorry, oh, so sorry," the Jade Emperor said. "The twelve winners have already been chosen."

The cat stormed and raged. She lunged for the rat whose treachery she vowed to repay. The rat sensed he was in mortal danger. Scurrying in and out among the grasses, he managed to elude the cat's grasp.

But the cat never forgot and never forgave. From that day on, she has relentlessly stalked her enemy, determined to pursue him to the ends of the earth.

The
Secret
in
the Moon
Cake

Early in the thirteenth century, a great horde of mounted Mongol
warriors thundered across China's northern border. They sacked
cities, plundered villages, laid waste the countryside, leaving in
their path numberless dead. In those fearful days a brave man
came forth who inspired his countrymen to cast out their barbarian conquerors and set free their beloved homeland.

Ju Yuan-jang, the son of a poor peasant family, was a simple
priest, piously devoted to his Buddhist faith. Given to long periods of quiet prayer and meditation, he hardly seemed likely to
become a great leader of men. Yet, when he could no longer
witness the agony of his people, he exchanged his priestly robes
for a soldier's uniform and took up arms. Faithful to his humble,
peasant beginnings, he was always modest in dress and speech,
and for this the soldiers of his secretly organized rag-tag army
loved him. They called him General Ju, and they would have
given up their lives willingly at his bidding.

For twelve long years General Ju never faltered in his fight to
drive the hated Mongols from Chinese soil. With every battle he
fought, his fame spread, north, south, east, and west, until there
was not a man who had not heard of his daring exploits. He is best
remembered for the recapture of the walled city of Feng Yang, an
unimaginable feat against impossible odds.

Behind the city loomed a tall mountain range, while in front of
it ran a wide, fast-flowing river. To mount an attack across the

river would mean the loss of many lives. His men could easily be spotted by the Mongol guards who patrolled from the top of the city walls day and night. If he were to attempt an assault from the mountains, his soldiers could be trapped in a narrow pass with all chance of escape cut off.

General Ju assigned the task of developing a strategy to his chief aide, Liu Bowen, while he kept his troops at the ready in the thickly wooded ridge above the city. Liu was a wise and loyal comrade. His quiet nature concealed an iron will and a brave heart.

For many hours Liu remained alone in his tent trying to design a plan of attack that had a good chance of succeeding. But in order to gain the upper hand over the enemy, he had to know what conditions were like inside the city, for without this vital information, even the best plan was doomed.

"I have decided to enter the city myself," Liu announced to General Ju. "It is the only way I can determine the strength of the Mongol garrison. More importantly, I want to find out how the people are faring and if we can count on their help should we need it."

"But that is a risky thing to do," General Ju protested. "How do you expect to gain entry into the city when all who pass through the gates are carefully checked by the watchful guards?"

"I have thought of that, and it may not be as difficult as you think. I shall go disguised as an ordinary peddler carrying a sack of leeks on my back. Those fools will never suspect a thing."

General Ju was not as optimistic as Liu. "Why must you go yourself? Send one of your trusted soldiers."

"It is a job that must be done with great care. One false step, and the Mongols will show no mercy."

Liu's passage through the city gates went smoothly. A guard ordered him to open his sack; then, satisfied that it had nothing in it but strong-smelling leeks, waved him on.

Once inside the city, Liu Bowen made his way to the market-

Liu called out to customers to come and buy.

place. "There," he reasoned, "I shall be able to speak to many people." The crowds were so thick he had trouble finding a spot to set down his sack of leeks. Farmers who had brought in their produce from the countryside hawked their wares at the top of their voices. With small children in their arms, women bargained loudly with the merchants. To occasional shouts of "Clear the way!" wooden-wheeled carts pulled by men or hitched to small donkeys rumbled across the stone pavement, adding to the clamor. Liu opened his sack, and imitating the others, called out to customers to come and buy. His sales were slow. Shoppers stopped to ask for several leeks, then haggled with him over the price before counting out a few coins. That they had little money to spend was obvious. Liu tried to engage them in conversation, but since the marketplace was constantly under the watchful eyes of Mongol soldiers, people seemed afraid to speak.

Toward the end of the day when Liu's sack was still half full, a poorly dressed man stopped to buy a few leeks. While the man fished in his pockets for the money to pay for his purchase, Liu observed him closely.

"Do you not go by the name Chang Li-bo?" he asked.

Surprised, the man answered, "Yes, that is my name."

"And did you not years ago reside in the village of Fu Shan?"

The man looked puzzled, but only for a fleeting moment, for all at once he recognized his boyhood friend. This chance meeting would prove to be a stroke of mutual good luck.

After exchanging greetings and news of their families, Chang invited Liu to his house, and Liu happily accepted the invitation.

Chang lived in a poor section of the city. The small homes, most consisting of only two rooms, were built close together along a narrow dirt street. Chang introduced his wife and fifteen-year-old daughter. He offered Liu a chair near the table. Over a cup of tea, Liu questioned his friend about life in the city under the Mongol occupation. Chang was glad for the opportunity to express his feelings freely to someone he could trust.

"Life has been very bitter. The coarse Mongol soldiers have no respect for us, not even for the elderly. When they are drunk they roam through the streets, shaming women by their crude language. On market days, in broad daylight, they snatch anything that catches their fancy, never paying the shopkeepers."

"Is there nothing that can be done to stop them?" Liu asked.

"Nothing, unless you are willing to die in the attempt. I, myself, observed what happens if one dares to resist. A Mongol barbarian tried to help himself to some fruit from a stall and the owner protested. The Mongol kicked over the stall, scattering the fruit, drew his sword, and with one thrust killed the poor man on the spot."

Chang lowered his head, afraid that his eyes would spill over and he would cry like a woman. But he had more to tell. "At the beginning of the new year, the Mongol general issued a new decree that was the harshest blow yet. One out of every twenty families was ordered to quarter a Mongol soldier. Not only must he be provided with food and lodging, but his requests, no matter how unreasonable, must be obeyed without question. My neighbors and I drew lots, and to my great sorrow, it fell upon me to provide a room for one of these Mongol soldiers. We had to give up our sleeping chamber and the three of us live cramped together in a single room. My wife tries to prepare tasty meals, but in return receives only complaints and abuse. Worse still, I fear for my daughter's safety. We pray each day that a Chinese army will come to our rescue."

Chang's unhappiness stirred Liu's determination to sweep the Mongols out of China and rid the land of their tyranny. "Help may be at hand," he told his friend. Beyond that he revealed only that a Chinese army was at that very moment encamped outside the city, and that he, Liu Bowen, was on a mission for General Ju to learn about the Mongol garrison. Swearing Chang to secrecy, Liu left and walked through the city gates just before they were locked for the night.

All the way back to camp he tried, without success, to think of some course of action. He could only report to General Ju what he had seen in the city and what Chang had told him about the Mongol oppressors.

The two men sat outside the general's tent weighing the possibility of one battle plan after another. It was already late, but neither General Ju nor Liu Bowen could sleep. A lantern moon hung overhead causing the trees to cast long, wavering shadows. Liu Bowen leaned back and gazed at the heavens.

"Of course!" he said, springing to his feet and breaking the stillness. "I'm sure it will work. The Mid-Autumn Festival will be celebrated in a few days, and everyone will be eating moon cakes."

"What are you muttering about?" asked General Ju, who was startled by Liu's sudden outburst. He did not understand why his normally sensible aide was talking about moon cakes when he himself was thinking of the best way to storm the city.

"Those barbarian Mongols will get just what they deserve." Liu pronounced this judgment as though he were an oracle predicting the future. A smile crossed his face. "And they will never be able to understand how we outwitted them," he added, still enjoying his private joke. Liu Bowen moved his stool closer to the general so he could speak without being overheard, and explained his strategy step by step.

"A brilliant idea," agreed General Ju. "We shall proceed at once to implement your plan."

For the next two days, while Ju's soldiers idled away the slowly passing hours, the army cooks worked feverishly without respite. They mixed and kneaded and baked thousands of moon cakes. The last batch to come off the stoves were decorated with a bright red mark the size of a pea. When the cakes were finished and cooled they were packed in four large carrying buckets. The day before the Mid-Autumn Festival, three of General Ju's bravest men were assigned to accompany Liu Bowen. They all appeared at the city gates dressed in dirty, ill-fitting pants and raggedy jackets full of patches. Like ordinary poor peddlers, each carrying a basket strapped to his back, they walked through the city gates without arousing suspicion. Once they reached the central market square they quickly set up a stall. They arranged three baskets on a makeshift counter and hid the fourth underneath. The smell of the freshly baked pastries with their delicious sweet bean-paste filling soon attracted many buyers. Whenever someone bought a few cakes, one of the soldiers would reach under the stall, pick up a cake with a red mark on it and offer it to the buyer.

"This is a bonus for you," he would say graciously. "It has a very special filling which you will surely like. May you be blessed with good fortune on the day of the Mid-Autumn Festival." The brisk activity around the stall aroused the interest of some Mongol guards. When they approached, Liu Bowen generously offered them a few cakes without charge. The ill-mannered soldiers repaid the kindness by grabbing as many as they could from the counter. They walked away without the least expression of thanks, and, of course, without the bonus.

Later in the day Liu's old friend Chang stopped to buy some cakes. Liu signaled to him not to speak, and quickly led him to one side. "You are probably surprised to see me once again in the guise of a peddler. This time, my good friend, my mission is different. I have come to free the city. Please accept this bag of moon cakes as a gift from General Ju. You will find one marked with a red dot. Open it as soon as you return to your house. You will know what to do. More I cannot tell you."

Most who received the extra cake were so curious about its special filling they did not wait until the day of the festival to taste it. After the first bite, it seemed no different from any ordinary moon cake, but with the second and third taste they bit into something with a strange texture. They discovered a tiny piece of rolled paper containing a written message: "On the evening of

Wave after wave of Chinese fighters charged through the gates.

the Mid-Autumn Festival, when you see bonfires in the hills above the city, kill the Mongol soldier in your house. Prepare to receive the righteous army.''

Quick as the wind word flew through the city. The Mongols had long ago seized all swords, daggers, cudgels, anything that might be a threat to their safety. But the Chinese people armed themselves with fence staves, large stones, even long-handled heavy pots.

On the day of the festival the very air seemed to crackle with excitement. The shopkeepers closed their shops earlier than was their custom and hurried home. The streets, normally teeming with people, were empty by early evening, with the exception of the Mongol guards on regular patrol.

The Mongol general sensed something unusual in the pulse of the city; still, he was not alarmed. ''They are busy preparing for their festival,'' he explained to his men. ''Let them have their foolish holiday as long as they do not cause trouble.''

Just after nightfall huge fires broke out in the hills. It was the signal to mount the attack. The Mongol soldiers quartered in Chinese homes never had a chance to escape, so quickly were they put to death.

After completing his mission Chang was one of the first to appear on the street. Unmindful of his own safety, he fought his way toward the city gates, cutting down any Mongol soldier who dared to block his way. The pent-up fury that had simmered for so many years during the Mongol occupation was suddenly unleashed. People poured out of their homes carrying any sort of weapon at hand, and within minutes the streets were littered with Mongol bodies.

The Mongol general made a final attempt to control the chaos. So many of his men had been slain he ordered the guards patrolling on top of the city walls to leave their posts and join the fighting below.

This was the chance that General Ju and Liu Bowen hoped for.

Tall ladders were speedily brought up and placed against the wall. Some of Ju's most daring men scurried to the top, pulled up the ladders and swung them over to the other side. While the battle raged, Chang managed to reach the city gates. He flung open the heavy timbered doors, welcoming Liu and his troops. Wave after wave of Chinese fighters charged through, overwhelming the Mongols. Their general surrendered and was led away in chains.

Throughout China people hailed the brilliant victory, for the Mongol yoke had been broken at last, and despair gave way to rejoicing. To this day it is said that the capture of the walled city was a master stroke. With the land free at last, General Ju, the former son of a peasant family, rose to even greater glory. He was seated on the Imperial Throne. As the first Ming Emperor, the dynasty he founded lasted for three hundred fruitful years.

Today, as they have done for centuries, Chinese people eat moon cakes during the Mid-Autumn Festival. It is customary to decorate them with a dash of red coloring in honor of General Ju's great victory. To eat a moon cake is a double treat. The delicious sweetness of the filling satisfies the taste. The symbol of the red mark satisfies the soul, for it is a reminder of the sweetness of liberty.